The Complete Instructional Baseball Manual

by

Fred Stanley

and

Lynn Stanley

Published by Phoenix Books for The Stanley Company, Inc.

ISBN #0-914778-64-1

THE COMPLETE INSTRUCTIONAL BASEBALL MANUAL *is a thorough and easily understood text which is sure to be a hit with players and coaches alike. I can't think of a single fundamental which isn't covered and carefully explained in this detailed instructional guide. It's complete, right down to graphic instructions for the execution of nearly every possible defensive situation. It's a learning tool as essential to amateur coaches and players as the right glove or the proper bat. It's unique, timeless and complete in every aspect of the game.* THE COMPLETE INSTRUCTIONAL BASEBALL MANUAL *covers all the basics of good, sound baseball.*

—Billy Martin
One of the most successful
Major League Managers of all
time; 4-time Manager of the Year.

For Florence and Blair Stanley

Without their encouragement and devotion, Fred's dream may have never become a reality.

And for Tracie and B. J.,

. . . who are the inspiration for everything we do.

"The difference between success and failure is doing a thing right and doing it exactly right."

—Edward Simmons

TABLE OF CONTENTS

THE BASEBALL MANAGER/COACH

A manager is more than just a "coach" to his players. At times, he will be forced to become a disciplinarian, a father, a teacher, a motivator and a friend.

As a coach, it is up to you to set an example for your kids to follow. In the lower classifications, this means that you must teach sportsmanship as well as mechanics. Keep your temper under control and conduct yourself in a sportsman-like manner both on and off the field. Avoid arguing with umpires—you only encourage your players to do the same thing. Be a coach that your kids can admire, a role model for them to follow.

The player's desire to win is directly related to his feeling for you as an individual. Earning the player's respect should be a primary concern of every dedicated manager. *Don't lie to your players;* they won't admire someone they cannot trust. Tell them the truth regarding their status on the team. If the player's ability is at issue, you only compound an already difficult situation by putting the player off. Further, your players deserve to know the truth; you would not tolerate a player who lies to you, so give your players the same consideration.

Make it clear from the beginning what you expect—and what you demand—from your players. Don't take anything for granted. Be consistent and fair with your players; once they know that you are *firm but fair,* they will respond in kind. *Always give your players the same respect that you want from them.*

In being fair, make sure that any rules you establish apply to *all* players. Though some of them may not agree with the rules you set down, they will admire your consistency in discipline.

Maintain your own health and physical appearance. You cannot credibly emphasize the importance of good physical conditioning if you yourself are overweight and out of shape.

Know all the rules of baseball.

COACHING 3RD BASE

There are no hard-and-fast rules for coaching 3rd base; a good 3rd base coach relies primarily on his instincts and must consider the following factors:

THE NUMBER OF OUTS
THE INNING
THE SPEED OF THE RUNNER
THE POSITION OF THE OUTFIELDERS
HOW HARD, AND WHERE THE BALL WAS HIT
THE STRENGTH OF THE OUTFIELDER'S ARM

With a runner in scoring position, most 3rd base coaches will try and pick up the baserunner's jump.* *Don't* look right away to see what jump he gets. Stay with the ball. *Concentrate on the ball, not the runner.*

As a rule—and again, this will vary depending on the game situation, if the runner reaches the bag before the outfielder has the ball, send him. If there is a runner at 2nd and no outs, hold the runner if you have any doubts at all. With one out, you have an option. With two outs, you send the runner.

With a runner at 2nd and the ball hit hard to the outfield, think *"stop"*, but don't signal *"stop"*. Get way down the 3rd base line and *watch the ball.* What the outfielder does with the ball will aid you in making the right decision. Don't get too close to 3rd base. *Keep your distance from the bag and off the line.*

With a runner at 3rd with one or no outs, have the runner shorten his lead; the runner cannot be doubled off in this situation.

When giving the signals, get up in front of the box so all runners can see your signs. If there is any doubt at all, *stop, get the hitter out of the box and start over.* If a player misses a sign, it is the 3rd base coaches fault! It is your responsibility to make sure that he has the sign; if that means jumping onto the field and yelling at the player, then do it!

*Leading off is not permitted in Little League.

2

Any hand signal should also be given verbally. Make sure the runner at 2nd understands what you want him to watch for. Make him give the number of outs back to you.

A very difficult play for a 3rd base coach is with a runner at 1st and 3rd and one or no outs. This is purely a judgement decision. If the ball is hit hard, you send the runner home. If the ball is merely topped, keep the runners at 3rd. It's better to have runners at 2nd and 3rd than at 1st and 2nd." One way to help the runner in this situation is to tell him *not to break hard his first two steps.* This will help him judge the speed of the ball and the direction that it is going.

Here are some things a good 3rd base coach should know:

1. Get in front of the box to give the sign.

2. After the hitter reaches 1st base and becomes a baserunner, you should get his attention *and* the attention of the hitter. Give your signs, *up in front of the coach's box.* After you give the sign, you should:

Alert the baserunner to locate the outfielders. If a soft line drive is hit, he can judge it better and get a good jump.

Tell the runner at 1st to watch a line drive; you don't want him to get picked off and ruin the inning.

Tell the runner not to let the 2nd baseman tag him on a slow roller to second base. Have him stop or slide into the 2nd baseman so he can't complete the double play.

Tell the runner to concentrate on making a good turn at 2nd base and to pick you up if he needs help.

Try to stay about 6' from the 3rd base bag in either direction so if the runner looks for you, he can pick you up easily.

3. With runners at 1st and 2nd:

Give the signs in front of the box. *Make sure everyone can see your sign!*

Runners should be aware of where the outfielders are playing. This will enable them to get a good jump on a soft liner or a ball in the gap.

3

Again, alert the baserunners to a line drive.

Tell the runner at 1st to watch the runner in front of him so he won't over-run him. On a double steal, it is his responsibility to go when the runner at 2nd goes.

Alert the runner at 1st that he should not allow the 2nd baseman to tag him.

Tell the runner at 2nd to make a good turn at 3rd. (You do this vocally, and by pointing at the 3rd base bag.)

With no outs and a long fly ball, have both runners tag up. This is a judgement play on the part of both runners, but *especially* at 1st. You *cannot* have your runner at 1st thrown out at 2nd for a double play! *He must watch the flight of the ball!*

Position yourself *at least* 15' from the bag towards home. This will help you make the decision to send the runner home or stop him. The farther you are down the line, the longer you have to either send the runner or hold him up. *Remember:* Don't watch the runner! *Stay with the ball!* You should already know who's running, what inning it is, what the score is, the number of outs and the strength of the outfielder's arms. All of these factors will aid you in your decision to send or hold a runner.

If you decide to send the runner, use your arms in a big circular motion, and yell at him; *you have to score!* BE VOCAL! You *must* be certain that he understands you. Once you've sent the runner home, hurry back to 3rd to help the runner rounding 2nd.

4. With 1 out:

If the ball is hit very high and deep and you're 100% sure that the ball will be caught, have the runner tag up. Otherwise, the runner will go as far down the line as he can and still get back safely if the ball is caught. The term most widely used is: "Go half way!" I would rather see a baserunner go as far as he thinks he can. In some cases, the runner at 1st can go right to the bag at 2nd.

5. With a runner at 2nd:

Give the sign in front of the box so both the hitter and the runner can see it clearly.

Let the runner know how many outs there are.

4

Alert him to where the outfielders are playing.

Tell him to watch for the line drive.

With one or no out, the runner must be sure that any ground ball hit to his right goes through the infield before he comes over to 3rd.

If the ball is hit to his left, he should advance to 3rd.

The runner should watch the pitcher. You will let him know if any of the middle infielders are moving toward him.

Be consistent with your verbal warnings. For example: "You're all right", "He's right behind you", "Get back!", etc. By being consistent, the runner will know how close the SS or 2nd baseman is to him.

On a long fly ball to the outfield, tell the runner to tag.

Tell the runner to make a good turn at 3rd.

Be will up the line towards home. Remember: The farther up the line you are, the easier it is to stop or advance the runner.

STAY WITH THE BALL, don't watch the runner! The status of the ball in the outfield or during the relay will help you make your decision regarding the runner.

THE MANAGER/COACH RELATIONSHIP

Your coaches should be indispensable. Delegate responsibility to them, they are qualified to handle it.

Be specific with your coaches regarding their duties. Make it clear what you expect from them and then have the confidence in them to let them do their jobs.

Your coaches should know that you demand their loyalty. Under no circumstances should your coaches second-guess you. Coaches must *never* discuss confidential matters with players or anyone else.

Loyalty and unity are foremost in the manager-coach relationship.

TIPS FOR HANDLING PITCHERS

It is important for managers and coaches to know their pitchers individually. What specific problems do they have? What are their strengths and weaknesses? What does it take to motivate them as individuals?

Just as there are no two hitting styles alike, there are no two pitching styles alike. Every pitcher has a "natural" way of throwing. By placing your pitchers in the outfield and hitting balls to them, you can easily determine the pitcher's natural throwing motion by studying him as he returns the ball to you.

Good strategy and a winning pitcher go hand-in-hand. Make sure your pitchers *know the hitters*. Discuss mistakes and work hard with your pitchers. Stress the mental preparation necessary before going to the mound. (See "Mental Preparation for Pitchers")

Teach your pitchers to field their position. They must know where to go on defensive situations. They must know how to hit, bunt, and run the bases effectively. It's not enough just to get the ball over the plate; pitchers should be *complete players*, educated in *every aspect* of the game of baseball.

Be careful not to overuse young pitchers with good arms. If you use such a pitcher too often, you run the risk of ruining his arm. In higher classifications, if you use relievers two nights in a row, it's a good idea to rest them for a couple of days.

The pitcher runs the ball game and should be alert to all game situations. He must always know the inning, the number of outs, the runners on base and the hitter at the plate.

Teach your pitchers to think *"low and hard"* and to pitch *in and hard.*

A good pitcher must:

MASTER THE FUNDAMENTALS
SACRIFICE
RUN HARD
BE DETERMINED
BE ABLE TO RECOVER FROM A LOSS

If a pitcher begins to lose control, it is your job to calm him down without destroying his confidence. If you notice him "tensing up", help him to relax and regain control. (See "Controlled Breathing Techniques")

The mound and the rubber are the pitcher's advantages. *Use them to their fullest.* The mound and the rubber are aids to the pitcher— the mound for height and the rubber for pushing toward the plate.

TIMING YOUR PITCHERS

When your pitcher is in the stretch position, take a stop watch and start it on his first movement. You stop the watch when the ball hits the catcher's glove. This constitutes the pitcher's time to the plate.

For example, in the Major Leagues, a good time to the plate for a righthanded pitcher is 1.30 seconds or less with a runner on 1st. With runners on 1st and 2nd, a good time is 1.35 seconds or less. Since there is less threat of a stolen base in this situation, the pitcher can take a little more time. More often than not, lefthanded pitchers are slower to the plate. They will try and hold, or fool the baserunner. A good time for a lefthanded pitcher in the Major Leagues is 1.40 with a runner on 1st; he should be quicker with a runner on 2nd—1.35 or better.

With a runner on 3rd, make sure your pitchers do the following:

CHECK THE RUNNER
GET THE SIGN
RE-CHECK THE RUNNER
MAKE THE PITCH

This method will help stop the forced balk. If the pitcher does not want to pitch out of the stretch, make sure he keeps his weight on the *pivot* foot. For example, righthanded pitchers should keep their weight on the left foot. Lefthanded pitchers should keep their weight on their right foot.

An important rule for every manager to know is this: *If you get your best reliever up, put him in the ball game.* If you warm him up and don't use him, you'll only tire him out and maybe decrease his effectiveness if you should need him later in the game.

SELECTING YOUR DEFENSE

THE CATCHER:

The catcher should be alert and aggressive. He should be able to "take charge", and should be able to run the game correctly. He should be gutsy and smart and have a strong, accurate throwing arm.

THE 1ST BASEMAN:

Every 1st baseman must have good hands. He must be able to handle low throws and short hops. He should have good control of his body and be able to coordinate movement of his feet.

THE 2ND BASEMAN:

He should have a good pair of hands and a strong throwing arm. He must be quick, alert and sure on his feet in all directions.

THE SHORTSTOP:

Shortstop is the most important position in the infield. The SS usually makes more plays than anyone else; he is the key to the defense on most teams. He must be alert and quick on his feet. He must have sure hands and a strong throwing arm and he *must know the hitters.*

THE 3RD BASEMAN:

The man at the "hot corner" must be quick to react to all game situations. He must have good hands, and a strong arm. He has to be able to charge in either direction and must be able to manage an off-balance throw with something on it to 1st base.

THE OUTFIELDERS:

All outfielders must be alert for all plays and have a strong, accurate throwing arm. They must be able to think quickly and must be aware of the game situation at all times. A good outfielder hustles 100% of the time. He should *back up every throw and base hit,* always assuming that the infielder will misplay the ball. He must be able to *throw the ball to the right place at the right time.*

THE LEFT FIELDER:

He usually has the weakest arm of all the outfielders. If possible, he should be lefthanded. This allows him to go into the left field foul area and catch the ball without having to back-hand it.*

CENTER FIELDER:

The center fielder should be one of your best athletes. He will probably cover the most ground. he must have a good arm. *Remember: You must be strong up the middle—shortstop, 2nd baseman and center fielder.*

8

RIGHT FIELDER:

He must have a good, strong arm and be righthanded if possible.*
This allows him to go into the right field foul line and catch the ball
without having to back-hand it.

*I know that some coaches will say that by having a lefthanded left
fielder or a righthanded right fielder the fielders will have to turn all
the way around to throw to 2nd base. Though that may be true in
some cases, it really depends on how fast the fielders are and how
hard the ball was hit. If the ball was hit hard enough for them to
turn all the way around, you can almost bet that the runner would
have been safe at 2nd anyway. By not having to back-hand the ball,
the outfielder may save a step and be able to eliminate the possible
triple or inside-the-park homerun.

ESTABLISHING A BATTING ORDER

The batters placed in front of the lineup will bat more often so,
naturally, you want your strongest hitters to bat first.

#1 BATTER: This batter is the "lead off man". He isn't
necessarily a "long ball" or homerun hitter, but should be a
player who gets on base consistently. He needs a good
knowledge of the strike zone and should not strike out often.

#2 BATTER: He will often be called upon to sacrifice. He
should be a good bunter and should be able to hit to right field
for a hit and run play. Hitting lefthanded would be a big asset;
he would block the catcher's view of 1st base, giving the runner an extra step. A lefthanded hitter can pull the ball in the
hole between 1st and 2nd and, if he has good speed, he can
reduce the chance of a double play.

#3 BATTER: He should be your most dependable hitter. As
he may often come to the plate in a double play situation, he
should have good speed, be a smart baserunner, and have fair
power.

#4 BATTER: The #4 batter is your "clean up man". He
should be a power hitter, able to clear the bases.

#5 BATTER: He will often come to the plate with runners in
scoring position. He should be a consistent hitter with some
power.

#6 BATTER: As the batting order progresses, the #6 batter may become your "lead off man" in later innings. He should be able to get on base. As he will often come to the plate with runners on, he should be able to hit for power.

#7 BATTER: He will frequently be in a position to advance runners into scoring position. He should be a good bunter, and should have occasional power.

#8 BATTER: As this hitter bats in front of the pitcher, who is usually your weakest hitter, he should have some speed so the pitcher can advance him with a bunt if he should get on base.

#9 BATTER: Your weakest hitter should bat in the #9 spot. However, this depends on whether or not you use the Designated Hitter Rule. If you do, insert the DH in the spot you feel he is best suited for. Otherwise, the pitcher generally hits in this spot.

In higher classifications, you may want to use right and lefthanded hitters, alternating in the order so that the opposing team is forced to use their entire bullpen.

TAKING INFIELD PRACTICE

The infield practice method described below is used by about 90% of all Major League teams:

OUTFIELD:

1. Hit 2 ground balls to left. The left fielder throws a one-hopper to the SS, who covers 2nd. The 2nd baseman backs up the SS.

2. Hit 1 ground ball and 1 fly ball to left. The left fielder throws home, a one or two-hopper to the catcher. Make sure he throws low enough so the 3rd baseman can cut it off. The SS covers 3rd, the 2nd baseman covers 2nd, etc.

3. Hit 2 grounders to the center fielder. He throws the ball low enough for the SS to cut it off. The SS should have his hands in the air and in a direct line to 3rd.

4. Hit 1 ground ball and 1 fly ball to center. The center fielder throws the ball at the cut off man's *chest.* Do not allow him to throw the ball all the way in the air. The ball should hit on the

home plate side of the pitcher's mound, *just past the dirt.*

5. Hit 2 ground balls to right field. The SS should be on the infield grass about 20-30' from 2nd, in *direct line* from right fielder and 3rd baseman, with hands in air. Right fielder hits SS in the *chest* with the ball. (Throw LOW)

6. Hit 1 ground ball, 1 fly ball. Right fielder throws a strike to 1st baseman (cut-off man—who is even with the pitcher).

INFIELD—GET ONE:

1. Hit 1 ground ball at each position. After they throw to 1st, they go to the bag and receive a throw from the catcher.

2. Hit a ground ball directly at the 3rd baseman. He throws to 1st. The 1st baseman throws home and the catcher throws to 3rd. Have the 3rd baseman make a *tag,* then throw to 2nd, where the 2nd baseman turns a double play.

3. Hit a ground ball to the SS. He throws to 1st. The 1st baseman throws to the catcher, who throws to 2nd. The SS makes a *tag* and then throws to 3rd. The 3rd baseman throws home.

4. Do the same drill for the 2nd baseman.

5. Hit a grounder to the 1st baseman. He fields the ball and throws to the SS who touches the bag as if he were turning a double play. The SS throws back to 1st, the 1st baseman covers the bag and then throws home.

6. Toss the ball away from the catcher as if it were a bunt. He races for the ball and throws to 1st. The 1st baseman throws to the SS at 2nd base. The SS throws *home,* not to 3rd. Repeat the same procedure, only hit the ball to right this time.

INFIELD—GET TWO:

1. Hit one ball up the middle and one to the right, following the same procedure as before. This time, the catcher throws to 2nd for a double play.

2. After two double play rounds, hit the last round forcing each player to go far to his right. Example: The 3rd baseman should field the ball almost on the line, and the 2nd baseman almost behind 2nd base.

11

3. No throw from the catcher. For the last ground ball, you can either have the infield charge slow rollers and throw to 1st, or you can have the infield in with the throw going home. If you can, hit the catcher a pop fly.

SELECTING THE PROPER EQUIPMENT

OUTFIELD:

The outfielder usually uses a glove with longer fingers. This gives him an extra inch or two on ground balls and a little added reach on balls hit over his head. The fingers are normally pulled fairly tight, which helps him hold on to the ball.

INFIELD:

3rd BASEMAN: He usually uses the biggest glove in the infield. His glove can be longer and deeper than either the SS or the 2nd baseman. The fingers are pulled tightly, helping him snag line drives. Tight fingers also aids the fielder in back-handing ground balls.

SHORTSTOP: His glove is usually just a little shorter and not as deep in the pocket as the 3rd baseman's. The SS must be sure handed; he doesn't have the luxury of being able to knock the ball down before throwing the runner out.

2ND BASEMAN: The 2nd baseman uses the smallest glove in the infield. It not only has the shortest fingers, it has the flattest pocket. The flat or shallow pocket enables the 2nd baseman to get the ball out of his glove quickly and throw to 1st base with one fluid motion.

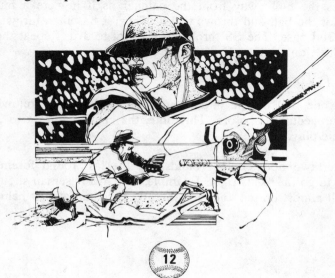

WHEN TO TAKE A PITCH

When to have a player take a pitch is an individual decision which changes with every hitter. Basically, if you have your best base-stealer on 1st and he breaks for 2nd, the batter should swing through the ball. By swinging through, or bunting, the catcher must stay back; this will give your baserunner an added step.

If it's late in the game, you're behind by a run or two, and you have your 7th, 8th or 9th batter up, I would say that you might want to have them take a strike—the pitcher may just walk one or two of them! The best way for a player to get a walk is to get right on top of the plate and crouch down; this reduces the strike zone. Many pitchers will start aiming the ball because they are afraid they will hit the batter.

About 90% of the time, if the first batter in the inning hits the first pitch for an out, the second batter should take a pitch. You don't want two pitches and two outs; you want to give your own pitcher a chance to catch his breath. This is especially true if the opposing pitcher is in a groove and yours is struggling.

When a hitter has three balls and no strikes, it's usually a good idea to have him take a pitch, (unless you have a homerun hitter at the plate). In this situation, most batters get over anxious and instead of waiting for a good pitch to hit, they swing at something they can't hit hard anyway.

13

PRACTICE SESSIONS

The manager sets the tone during practice sessions. If you are full of enthusiasm and encouragement for your players, it will rub off on them. If I had to offer one piece of advice for a successful practice session, it would be this: *Be organized!* Don't let your players stand around. Let the pitchers hit ground balls to the infielders and fly balls to your outfielders. All infielders should take at least 50 ground balls per session; they should field ground balls to their right and left and with the infield in. The SS and 2nd baseman should work on double plays, the 1st and 3rd basemen should work on charging for a bunts and slow rollers. The catcher should work on blocking balls in the dirt, throwing to 2nd, catching pop-flys. Outfielders work on charging ground ball *hard* and fielding them cleanly.

If you are organized, a one-hour practice session three times a week is plenty for Little Leaguers; anything longer than that and your team will show it on the field. In higher classifications, coaches must determine what is reasonable. However, on all levels, I encourage coaches to be consistent; if you tell players and parents that a session will end at six o'clock, *end it* at six o'clock.

Encourage your players to hustle 100% if the time. Never allow players to walk on or off the playing field. Players who don't hustle during practice should be disciplined. And, in the case of Little Leaguers, stress the importance of keeping with the flow of the game and knowing play situations. Encourage young ballplayers to use their time on the bench to study the game and the hitters.

Coaches should have a routine set-up for conducting batting practice. Here is an example:

1. Bunt—one down 1st, one down 3rd.

2. Hit and run.

3. Now the batter must hit the ball to the right side of the diamond to advance the runner from 2nd to 3rd.

4. Fly ball—hit a sacrifice fly.

5. Squeeze bunt.

6. Batter takes 5 swings.

This routine makes the batter think about game situations and makes the baserunner concentrate on what he should do on the basepath.

Don't allow your team to just go through the motions during practice sessions. *How you practice is how you'll play.*

"Perfect practice makes perfect play."

CONDITIONING

Too often, players put strenuous demands on their bodies without the proper preparation. In the minor leagues especially, the travel schedule (usually on busses), did not allow us enough time to really loosen up before a game. *Poor pre-game warm up is the cause of most baseball injuries.* Good physical conditioning will minimize strains, muscle pulls and shin-splints. A twenty to thirty minute warm up period is recommended prior to each game and work out. The stretching exercises described on the following pages are designed to condition the muscles most frequently used in baseball.

It is imperative that these stretching exercises are done carefully, "eased into". *Do not bounce or overstretch. Do not start or stop quickly. Go at your own pace.* Eight-counts are recommended for these exercises as follows:

1-2 begin the stretch,
3-4 *ease* into the stretch,
5-6-7 Reach your maximum position and hold to 8.

STRETCHING EXERCISES

STRETCHING THE CALF MUSCLES:

Done religiously, this exercise nearly eliminates the possibility of shin splints (tightness of the calf muscle which causes pain to the front of the leg.)

1. Stand with feet hip-width apart, toes slightly "pigeon toed", weight on the outsides of the feet.

2. Lean against a wall with feet apart, (about 18" from the base of the wall), and with a slight stretch on the calf muscle.

3. Lean forward, bending elbows just enough to slightly increase the stretch in the calf muscle. *Keep heels on the ground and do not strain.* Hold for 10 seconds. Repeat 10 times.

The calf muscle stretch takes only about 3 minutes and should be done three times a day during the playing season. As the muscle becomes more flexible, move the feet farther out from the wall. Used frequently, this exercise will eliminate any tightness in the calf.

From a squat position, stretch the right leg straight out to the side. Lean toward your right foot. Hold 8 seconds and repeat with the opposite leg.

Repeat as above, toes pointing up this time.

SHOULDER EXERCISES:

The Roll: Arms outstretched, start with small circular motions forward, gradually increasing the size of the circles. Reverse. Do 8 reps.

Circles: With arms at your sides, make large circular motions, first forward and then reverse. Do 8 reps.

Hugs: Arms outstretched, "Hug" yourself, slapping your shoulder blades. Return your arms to the outstretched position. Do 8 reps.

Shoulder Stretch:

1. With arm overhead, hold your elbow with your opposite hand, pulling gently. Hold 8 seconds.

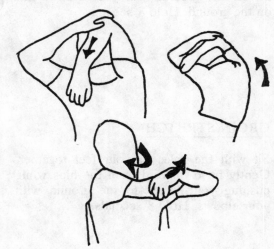

2. Gently pull to the opposite side while bending at the waist. Hold 8 seconds.

3. Gently pull your elbow across your chest, toward the

17

opposite shoulder. Hold 8 seconds.

TRUNK ROTATIONS:

With hands stretched in front of your chest, rotate upper body right and left. Do not move your hips. 8 reps.

BACK FLEXION:

Lying prone, lift legs and chest off the ground at the same time. Return to a flat position. Do 12 reps.

BENT KNEE SIT UPS:

Lay on the ground, knees slightly bent and hands behind your head. Pull up, *keeping your elbows back.* Use your stomach muscles *not your arms,* to pull yourself up. Go back half way, and don't let your head touch the ground. 25 reps.

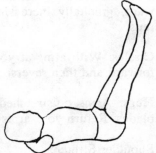

LEG LIFTS:

Lay down, legs straight. Lift legs up to a 90 degree angle and lower them to about 3" off the ground with your elbows flat on the ground. Hold 8 seconds.

GROIN STRETCH

Sit with the soles of your feet together. Gently bend forward from the hips while pushing your knees to the ground with your elbows. Hold 8 seconds.

HIP STRETCH:

With left leg out in front, grab the right ankle with your left hand and pull up to the left shoulder. Right hand and forearm should be supporting the right knee. Hold 8 seconds; repeat to opposite side.

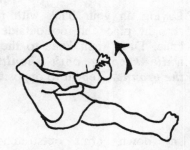

ACHILLES TENDON STRETCH:

In a semi-kneeling position, the toes of your right foot should be even with your left knee. The heel of the bent leg can come off the ground about 1". Lower your heel to the ground, *keeping it flat* while you push forward on your thigh with your chest and shoulder. Repeat, changing legs.

FOREARM STRETCH:

Arms straight out in front of you, grasp right hand with left and flex your wrist. Hold for 8 seconds and repeat with the opposite arm.

HAMSTRING STRETCH:

Put left foot slightly in front of the right and bend forward at the waist while keeping your right leg straight. Hold 8 seconds. Repeat, with your left foot forward this time.

BACK STRETCHES:

Sit with your left leg straight. Place right foot outside of left knee, and left elbow outside of right knee. Rotate lower trunk to the right while looking back as far as possible. Hold 8 seconds and repeat to the opposite side.

19

Laying on your back with right leg straight, place left foot outside of right knee. Drop right knee to the ground *while keeping both shoulders on the ground.* Repeat to opposite side.

Lay down, arms outstretched. Raise right leg, bringing right foot to your left hand. Alternate. 12 reps.

Lying down, pull left knee to chest. Hold 8 seconds and repeat with right knee.

Raise legs slowly over your head until your toes touch the ground. Point your toes and stretch. Hold 10 seconds. Relax, maintaining your position. Now, rest the balls of your feet on the ground and flex. Hold 10 seconds. Come down slowly, one vertebrae at a time.

QUADRICEP STRETCH:

Left leg extended out in front, sit with right leg bent, heel touching right hip. Bend backward, forcing your knee flat on the ground. Hold for 8 seconds, switch and repeat.

ABDOMINAL STRETCH:

Lying prone, grasp your ankles and pull up, lifting your chest and legs off the ground. Hold 8 seconds, repeat.

HIP FLEXOR STRETCH:

In a semi-squat position, force your hip downward. Hold 8 seconds. Switch legs and repeat.

SKY REACHES:

Stand with feet together. Keeping your legs straight, bend at the waist and touch the ground. Coming up on your tip-toes, reach to the sky, stretching from the waist. 15 reps.

Utility players are more susceptible to pulled and strained muscles because they do not play every day. They should run daily with the pitchers in addition to their stretching exercises. Remind these players of their importance; if there is an injury to one of your starters, the utility men must be ready at a moment's notice.

WEIGHT TRAINING

I feel this book would not be complete without a section on weight training. When I first signed in 1966, weight training was used primarily for football players, or for players who had been injured and were placed on rehab programs. If one did any weight lifting at all, it was done for the purpose of building endurance—lots of reps and very little weight.

When I first signed, I was 5'10" and weighed 150 lbs. By the time I had been playing six years of pro ball, I was 5'11" and weighed 160 lbs. If I had it to do over again, I assure you that I would lift weights to make myself stronger. I really feel that my career was cut short because I did not keep up with the times. Athletes today are bigger, stronger, faster and smarter. They are better in every aspect of the game than they were ten or twelve years ago. Had I lifted weights and become stronger, I'm sure that I could have driven the ball with more consistency. I honestly do not know a good hitter in the Major Leagues who does not have very strong hands, wrists, forearms, shoulders and legs. To create bat speed, you must have a strong upper body.

I have cited some weight programs which may aid you in becoming a better athlete. Though I strongly encourage the use of these programs, I cannot over stress the importance of professional super-

21

vision before undertaking *any* weight program. Professional strength coaches are trained to know the individual needs of each body type. The programs listed are merely suggestions for strengthening the specific portions of the body used in baseball.

The programs cited do not specify the amount of weight for each set. This was done purposely because everyone is not the same strength—what might be fine for you may be too heavy for your friend. Let a professional test you; he can tell what is a safe weight for you. *Remember: You can seriously injure yourself lifting weights if you don't know what you're doing. Don't be foolish and jeopardize your career.*

BEGINNER WEIGHT PROGRAM
AGES 10-14

Do this program twice a week, preferably on Monday and Thursday. Always do major lifts first.

1. Leg press—5 sets of 6 reps.

2. Knee extensions—5 sets of 8 reps.

3. Knee flexions—4 sets of 5 reps.

4 Incline dumbell press—5 sets of 5 reps.

5. Toe raises—3 sets of 5 reps.

6. Bent arm pullovers—5 sets of 5 reps.

7. Curls (dumbbells, bar or cables)—5 sets of 5 reps.

8. Tricep extensions (dumbbells, bar or universal latt pull bar)—5 sets of 5 reps.

9. Dips—3 sets of 15 reps.

10. Crunchies—3 sets of 15 reps.

11. Situps, twisting—one set of 50 twists each way.

22

INTERMEDIATE WEIGHT PROGRAM
AGES 15-16

Do this program three times a week, Monday, Wednesday and Friday. Always do major lifts first.

1. Leg press—6 sets of 8 reps.

2. Leg extensions—5 sets of 10 reps.

3. Leg flexions—4 sets of 5 reps.

4. Bench press—5 sets of 5 reps.

5. Military press (dumbbells)—5 sets of 5 reps.

6. Dumbbell or barbell curls—5 sets of 6 reps.

7. Tricep extensions (dumbbells, bar or universal latt pull bar)—5 sets of 5 reps.

8. Toe raises—3 sets of 20 reps.

9. Wrist rolls, forward and reverse—2 sets each way.

10. Finger squeezes and hand squeezes—Using a tennis or racquet ball, squeeze until the hands and forearms feel fatique.

11. Bent leg sit ups, twisting—1 set of 50 twists each way.

12. Side bends—50 each way.

13. Twisters—50 each way.

ADVANCED WEIGHT PROGRAM
AGES 17 AND UP

Do this program 3 times a week, Monday, Wednesday and Friday.

1. Squats—5 sets of 5 reps.

2. Incline press—5 sets of 6 reps.

23

3. Bent arm pullovers—5 sets of 6 reps.

4. Toe raises—3 sets of 25 reps.

5. Upright rows—5 sets of 5 reps.

6. Stiff leg deadlifts—3 sets of 25, 15, and 10 reps each.

7. Curls—(dumbbells or barbells)—5 sets of 8 reps.

8. Tricep extensions (dumbbells, bar or universal latt pull bar)—5 sets of 6 reps.

9. Wrist rolls, forward and reverse—3 sets each way.

10. Bent leg situps—3 sets of 25 reps.

11. Side bends (dumbbells)—75 each way.

AT-HOME WORKOUT

If you don't have easy access to a gym, here is a good workout you can do at home:

1. Toe raises: Bend your body in a 45 degree angle while resting your hands on a bench. Have someone sit on your lower back-buttock area. Raise your heels up with your toes in, out, and straight ahead.

2. Finger and hand squeezes: Squeeze a racquet or tennis ball until you can't squeeze anymore. Do 3 reps.

3. Finger pushups: Do as many pushups on your fingertips as you can.

4. Twisters: With a broomstick behind your neck, keep your body stationary from the waist down while twisting the upper body from right to left. Do 3 sets of 50.

5. Side bends: With a broomstick behind your neck, bend from side to side without moving your lower body. Do 3 sets of 25 to each side, alternating after each 25.

6 Hanging obliques: Hang from a chin-up bar so that your legs lift while your body twists.

7. Crunchies: Lay on the floor and bend your legs over a bench at your knees. Do 3 sets of 20 situps from this position.

8. Wrist rolls: Drill a hole in a rounded stick. (A broken bat works well if you saw off the handle. It should be about 12-15" long.) Run a cord through it and tie a knot in one end so the string will not come out. Tie the other end of the string to a barbell plate. Roll the cord up and then down, keeping your arms and elbows straight out in front of you. Roll *slowly.* Do 3 reps.

NUTRITION

The athlete's body is to him what a finely tuned race car is to a professional driver—it is impossible to operate at peak performance without a properly fueled body. A professional driver would never consider putting anything but the highest quality fuel into his car. The serious athlete must fuel his body with only the most nutritious foods. Twenty years ago, it was believed that a pre-game diet of high-protein, low carbohydrate foods was essential for optimum physical performance. However, all of the information available today proves contrary to that belief. Almost without exception, medical experts and athletes alike agree that carbohydrates should be the primary ingredient in the athlete's diet. Carbohydrates, or "glycogen", are stored in the muscle tissue. From there, they "feed" the muscle cells during physical activity. *It is a medical fact that, when glycogen runs out, physical exhaustion results.* Unfortunately, the body stores carbohydrates in only limited quantities. An inactive person carries about a six-hour supply of glycogen. Active persons must "refuel" by eating carbohydrates several times throughout the day. Nutritious carbohydrate foods include: White, and preferably whole-grain breads and cereals, potatoes and rice, pasta and fresh fruit.

WATER

Every bit as important as what we eat is what we drink. *Large amounts of water are essential for a healthy body.* Water regulates the body temperature and aids in eliminating toxic wastes; it supplies muscles and vital organs with oxygen and nutrients and helps to maintain proper volume and pressure of the blood. *Inadequate water supply is one of the primary causes of poor perfor-*

mance in any physical activity. Every athlete should make a conscious effort to think about his consumption of liquids. At least *1 quart* of water should be consumed for every 1,000 calories of food eaten.

As a general rule, three or more glasses of water should be consumed about three hours before a game. Another two glasses should be drunk from 15-30 minutes before. During a game, two glasses of water *per hour* are recommended.

Beverages such as iced tea and colas should be avoided before a game. These drinks are high in caffeine, which increases nervous tension and forces the heart to work harder. In addition, caffeine depletes water and salt from the body through increased urination. I am personally opposed to the use of colas or other carbonated sodas as beverage before a game. Besides being exceptionally high in sugar content, these drinks tend to cause gas and a bloated feeling.

Serious athletes should avoid the use of alcohol. Alcohol dehydrates cells and impairs muscle efficiency, coordination and mental judgment. *Alcohol should never be consumed before competition.*

REMEMBER: Water loss occurs constantly, and at an increased rate during physical activity. Water supply should be continually replenished throughout prolonged physical activity. *Don't wait until you're thirsty to drink!*

SALT

As we sweat, we lose salt from our bodies. Many athletes believe that salt tablets are necessary to replenish this loss. The truth is: *Salt tablets are dangerous.* They increase the level of salt at too fast a rate and distort the natural salt-to-water ratio in the body. The easiest, and safest way to replenish salt loss is by drinking water.

If athletes use caution in selecting the foods they eat, there should be no need for vitamin supplements. Basically, this means eating a well-balanced variety of food from the four basic food groups. However, most athletes require higher amounts of certain micronutrients than non athletes. Specifically, these are Potassium, Magnesium, and Thiamin.

26

Below are some suggested foods which are high in these nutrients:

POTASSIUM-RICH FOODS: Orange juice, bananas, dried fruits and unsalted nuts.

MAGNESIUM-RICH FOODS: Almond and cashew nuts, other unsalted nuts, meat, fish, whole-grain breads and cereals, milk and leafy green vegetables.

THIAMIN-RICH FOODS: Whole-grain breads and cereals, milk, eggs, organ meats and pork.

WEIGHT CONTROL

It should be obvious to everyone that an overweight athlete becomes fatigued more easily than one who is not. Excess weight effects speed and agility—elements essential to the game of baseball. Since the average athlete burns up at least 3,000 calories per day, a 2,000 calorie diet is recommended when weight loss is desired. At this rate, a loss of two pounds per week will result. It is inadvisable for an active athlete to lose weight at a faster rate than this.

For athletes who wish to gain weight, foods such as peanut-butter, whole-grain breads and cereals, raisins, bananas, and yoghurt are suggested as healthy snack foods.

PRE GAME MEALS

In considering what to eat before a game, keep in mind that the foods you eat must do the following things: 1) Provide energy and keep you from getting hungry during a game, 2) prevent gastrointestinal upset during the game and 3) be combined with the proper amounts of water to prevent dehydration. Avoid raw fruits which may cause gas and bulk foods such as raw vegetables (except lettuce), nuts, popcorn, seeds and other whole-grain foods before competition. It is best to eat 3-4 hours before the game; this allows time for your food to digest and aids in preventing gastrointestinal upset. As fats and proteins take a long time to digest, your pre-game meal should be low in fatty foods and high in carbohydrates. *Avoid sugar* before a game; it often causes acute hunger pangs hours after it is digested. Here is an example of a recommended pre-game meal:

2 oz. poultry or fish (not fried)
8 oz. skim milk
pasta or baked potato
banana
plain lettuce salad or cooked carrots
2 cups clear bouillon
oatmeal cookie or yoghurt

In summary, your pre-game meal should consist of 60% carbohydrate, 20% protein, 20% fat, and be less than 500 calories. At least one serving per day should be eaten from each of the following food groups:

Milk
Protein
Bread/Cereal
Vitamin C
Dark-Green Vegetables
Other Vegetables
Fresh Fruit

1. Limit your intake of fats.

2. Increase your intake of whole-grain products.

3. Eat only fresh fruits and vegetables whenever possible. If you can't get fresh, frozen are preferable to canned products, which are high in salt and preservatives.

4. Eat generous quantities of dark green vegetables—these are excessively high in folic acid, a compound necessary for production of red blood cells. Some of these vegetables are: Broccoli, Spinach, Romain and Red-Leaf Lettuce, and Fresh Green Beans.

5. Limit your use of fats such as butter, margarine, mayonaise, whole milk and ice cream.

The chart on the following page can be removed from this book and placed in your kitchen. It provides an excellent guide to the calories in foods and should be used when planning your menus.

"FREE FOODS"

Alfalfa Sprouts	Artichokes
Asparagus	Bean Sprouts
Broccoli	Brussel Sprouts
Cabbage	Celery
Cucumbers	Eggplant
Green Beans	Green Onions
Green Peppers	Greens
Lettuce	Mushrooms
Radishes	Spinach
Tomatoes	Zucchini
Plain Popcorn	Mineral Water
Vegetable Juice	Spices
Lemon	Vinegar

"LIGHT FOODS"

Non-Fat Milk	Pineapple
Low-Fat Milk	Oranges
Buttermilk	Carrots
Plain Yoghurt	Potatoes
Wheat Bread	Cottage Cheese
Fish	Puffed Wheat
Skinless Chicken	Shredded Wheat
Turkey	Corn Tortillas
Beans	Whole Grain Crackers
Peas	Oat Meal
Apples	Whole Grain Pasta
Bananas	Barley
Peaches	Brown Rice
Grapes	Grapefruit
Strawberries	

(See over for *"Heavy Foods"*)

"HEAVY FOODS"

Whole Milk
Flavored Yoghurt
Cheese
Beef, Pork, Lamb
Ham, Bacon
Luncheon Meats
Sausage
Waffles
Pancakes
Hot Dogs
Hamburgers
T.V. Dinners
Tacos
Fried Rice
Snack Crackers

Avacados
Peanut Butter
Raisins
Canned Fruit
Biscuits
Sweet Muffins
Salami
Fish Sticks
French Toast
Coffee Cake
Doughnuts
Sweetened Cereals
Burritos
Pizza
Creamed Soups

This list of *"Heavy Foods"* includes all foods high in sugar content.

RUNNING

Running is probably the single most important phase of good conditioning. It not only maintains physical fitness overall, it improves the functions of the circulatory and respiratory systems, thus increasing the stamina and endurance so necessary for athletes. Running strengthens the leg muscles and increases the flexibility of the body. I cannot overemphasize the importance of a daily running program for ballplayers.

If the desire is there, anyone can learn to run faster. In addition to the power running program outlined herein, I have listed some tips to aid players in running *correctly* in order to increase their speed.

1. Relax. In order to perform at optimum level, the body must be flexible and yielding.

2. *Run only on the balls of your feet.*

3. The toes should be pointed *straight ahead.* This can mean a difference of as much as ½ step on each stride.

4. Run in a *straight line.*

5. *Don't overstride.* Proper stride is about equal to the height of your body. It takes time to develop the proper stride. *Running must be practiced.*

6. The body should lean slightly forward, head up. Ankles, hips, shoulders and head should be in a straight line. *Don't lean backwards.*

7. *Use your arms.* Opposite arm and leg should move in unison.

Do short sprints to develop speed, distance running to develop endurance and running in circles to strengthen ankles, hips and back.

THE POWER RUNNING PROGRAM

This program was designed by Olympic Gold Medalist Herman Frazier. The basic principle behind the PRP is for the runner to generate a strong arm drive and a high knee lift. This program combines this technique with controlled breathing and muscle relaxation. It is an excellent running program and will aid in improving the

31

athlete's agility and power. Players who run the 40 yard dash in 4.6 should improve to 4.3 or 4.4 with any effort at all. You will see the results of the PRP if you time your players twice a month in the 40 yard dash.

Do these drills twice weekly throughout the season.

ARM DRIVE:

Do two 1-minute exercises.

1. Standing in place, keep elbows locked at a 90 degree angle.

2. Relax the hands. Thumb and index finger should be lightly touching.

3. Relax the facial muscles.

4. Arm motion:
Back Stroke—hands even with back pockets. Up Stroke—hands in front of nose.

SITTING DRILL:

1. Sit with legs fully extended in front of you. Have a partner hold your ankles.

2. Using *full range of motion and a good arm drive, go hard!* If done properly, you should bounce off your buttocks. Keep your facial muscles relaxed.

3. Do this exercise twice for 15 seconds, then twice for 20 seconds. Alternate with your partner.

RUNNING IN PLACE:

Do two 1-minute exercises, *emphasizing the arm drive and knee lift.*

CONTROLLED BREATHING—"POPS":

1. Inhale to start and hold your breath.

2. Exhale at 25 yards.

3. Inhale at 30 yards and hold until the finish (40 yards).

4. On 30 yards, inhale and quicken the arm drive; this is the "pop".

CARIOCA—SIDE RUN, CROSS OVER:

Start easy and smooth, with knees high. Do 4 times at 25 yards and walk back.

RUNNING BACKWARDS:

Go at 80-90%—do 3 times at 25 yards.

BOUNDING UP AND OUT:

Bound up into the air with exaggerated strides. Do 3 times at 25 yards.

Players should be timed twice a month in the 40 yard dash. In addition to the PRP, players should be able to run the mile in under 6 minutes. The long distance helps maintain the endurance necessary for a long and strenuous season.

CONTROLLED BREATHING TECHNIQUES

Disorganized thinking, anxiety or nervousness, can lead to shortness of breath, or "hyperventilation". This increases muscular tension throughout the body. As muscles tense, they become hard and contract. For example, the tighter a hitter grasps his bat, the stiffer his arms become.

The ability to control one's breathing is instrumental in easing the tension which accumulates in stress situations. Our breathing affects our coordination, timing, balance, and range of motion, as well as our tension level, accuracy and power. Every athlete who wishes to be successful must learn to control his pattern of breathing. This takes time and must be practiced. Below are a couple of exercises which may prove helpful in lowering the tension level. Ideally, these exercises should be done in a quiet atmosphere before too much tension accumulates. Again, these exercises *must be practiced.* Once they have been mastered, players will find it easy to relax and control their breathing at will.

FILLING THE LUNGS WITH CLEAN AIR:

Lay on your back in a relaxed position. Stretch out your arms and legs, close your eyes and take a deep breath, allowing your chest to fill with clean air. Imagine your chest is a balloon, "inflating" with air until it feels as if it will burst. Now, hold your breath until you begin to feel slight discomfort. Let the air out S L O W L Y and relax. Repeat.

MUSCLE TENSING:

In the same position, tense every muscle in your body, starting with your toes and feet. Tighten your shin and clave muscles, your knees, thighs and buttocks...tighten every muscle up to and including your jaw. Now, squeeze your eyes shut tightly and hold for several seconds. Release the tension slowly, feeling all of the tightness leave your body until every muscle is completely free and relaxed. Let out all of your breath and lay quietly, feeling the tingling sensation throughout your muscles. *Concentrate on slow, even breathing.* If done properly, once is enough for this exercise. However, if you still feel tension in your muscles, repeat it.

QUICKNESS AND AGILITY DRILLS

AGILITY SIDE STEP: In a period of 10 seconds, see how many side steps you can take: Alternate moving to the right and then to the left in a "shuffle", without crossing your feet. Weight should be on the balls of the feet, arms should hang losely at the sides. Repeat 5 times to each side.

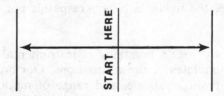

QUICK STARTS: The runner *explodes* from a stand-still position. Run forward 25 yards, accelerating as you go. Return the same way. Repeat, only this time *explode* again for another 25 yards. Return the same way. 5 reps.

"GO STARTS": The runner should be in a starting position, ready to "go" when the ball is hit. Feet should be hip width apart, weight on the balls of the feet, arms lose, body relaxed and glove open.

1. Cross the right foot over the left and go 4 steps, reaching for the ball with the glove hand, arm extended. *Drop the right foot behind the left* and come up throwing to 1st base with a

34

sidearm or ¾ action. Repeat 10 times.

2. Cross the left foot over the right, "sliding" into a plant position, left foot slightly in front of the right, about shoulder width apart. With your glove open, bring your hands toward your chest in a "fielding" motion. Shift your weight to your back foot, drop your arm back and throw the ball hard to 1st or 2nd base, being as quick and accurate as possible. Repeat 10 times.

3. "Bust" on a ground ball. Stay low, field the ball and take a quick shuffle step to regain your balance. Now, throw to 1st from close to the ground. Repeat this drill, throwing from about half way up the second time. *Your main objective here is to regain your balance quickly and get rid of the ball as fast as you can.* Repeat 10 times.

4. Imagine a pop fly is hit behind you. Drop the left foot back and move to your left. Run to a spot slightly further than where you think the ball is. Using your glove to shield the sun, try to catch the ball. Repeat to the right, dropping the right foot back. Repeat 10 times.

5. Skip rope, alternate speeds and turn left and right.

6. Throw balls against a wall and field them. Your glove should be open and in front of you, forming a triangle to each shoulder. Bring the glove back to your chest, regaining your balance with quick shuffle steps. Do this exercise for 15 minutes per day.

3

HITTING—BASIC FUNDAMENTALS

There are no two hitters who hit alike, just as there are no two golf or tennis swings exactly alike. Hitting is an individual thing, and hitting style must be developed by each individual batter. There are, however, some basic fundamentals and methods of training which can be taught and will aid young ballplayers in becoming better hitters.

BE COMFORTABLE

USE YOUR HANDS

DON'T USE TOO MUCH BODY

KEEP YOUR EYES ON THE BALL

PICK UP THE BALL FROM THE RELEASE POINT

As each player is physically and mentally different, it is difficult to say what hitting style is best for you. You must ask yourself:

1. Am I big and strong? Could I become a home run hitter?

2. Should I be a contact hitter—make the pitcher work? Should I try to hit the ball to all fields?

3. Should I attempt to become a good bunter to compensate for my lack of power? (Draw the infield in and try to hit ground balls past them?)

Once you have answered these questions, you can then select a bat and stance which will help you to become the type of hitter you want to be.

36

SELECTING THE PROPER BAT:

1. Select a bat that you can control throughout the entire swing.

2. Your strength and the amount of speed you can generate with the bat (through the strike zone) will determine the length and weight of the bat you should use.

3. Generally speaking, if you have small hands, you will be better off with a small-handled bat.

4. It is better to have a bat which is too light than one which is too heavy. A heavy bat can cause mechanical breakdown, which is hard to eliminate once it becomes habit—this is especially true for younger ballplayers. Also, a heavy bat must be started earlier in the swing; this does not give the hitter the luxury of being able to wait on the pitch. Heavy bats do not drive the ball any further than light ones—bat *speed* determines distance.

GRIP ON THE BAT:

The bat should be placed at the base of the fingers. If it is placed

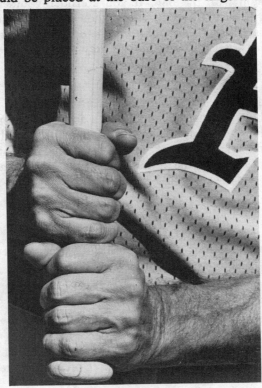

too far back in the palm of the hand, it will restrict good hand actions. A hitter who has the bat placed deep in the palm of his hand will have a tendency to "sweep" the bat, which retards bat speed.

Here is one method used to help a hitter get the bat into the base of of his fingers: Stand, placing the bat against your left leg. Bend down and put your left hand on the bat, placing it at the base of your fingers. Take your right hand and place it on top of your left. Now, pick up the bat. It should be placed exactly at the base of your fingers, with the middle knuckles somewhat aligned.

Physical strength cannot be overstressed. It takes strong hands, wrists, shoulders and legs to drive the ball consistently. Weaker hitters may want to flatten the bat; this will aid in shortening the stroke, thus making the bat quicker.

THE HANDS:

It's better to have your hands held at the top of the strike zone; this allows the hitter to move in only one direction with his hands—on a downward plain with the ball. If you consider yourself a homerun hitter, you will want to move your hands a little lower so you can get the ball in the air. *To achieve the maximum bat speed, the hitter's hands must go back before they come forward.*

THE STRIDE:

The stride should be made directly toward the pitcher just *after* he releases the ball. Your stride should be a soft "glide" on to your big toe. By touching your big toe to the ground, the soft glide will help you stay back on your *back* leg and will aid in eliminating the lunge. (Lunging makes the hitter susceptible to off-speed pitches.) Your hands, body weight and head should all remain *back* during the stride.

THE HIPS:

The hips should not start to open until the batter has seen the pitch. Your swing will automatically bring your hips through.

FRONT SHOULDER:

The front shoulder is the guide to the ball; it should always point to the ball until the swing actually occurs. *Keeping the front shoulder in is essential on breaking pitches.* If your front shoulder flies out too soon, you will pull off of the breaking pitch.

Anything off speed, or a ball breaking away from you will give you problems. You will also lose bat speed. When your shoulder flies out too soon, so does your head.

HEAD AND EYES:

The hitter should train his eyes to pick up the ball as soon as possible. The hitter should have a feeling of his head remaining *over* the ball during the swing. His head should be turned toward the pitcher so the hitter can see the pitcher with *both* eyes. (Head comes back and down with the pitch—the eyes alone cannot track the flight of the ball.)

WEIGHT DISTRIBUTION:

The hitter must keep his body weight on the balls of his feet. About 70% of the weight should be on his back foot. *Power and stability come from hitting off of the back foot.* The weight will transfer from the back to the front foot through the hips (not the shoulders), as the bat comes forward through the ball.

STANCE:

Your position in the batter's box will aid you in achieving optimum plate coverage and is important in determining the type of hitter you will become. The further back in the box you stand, the more time you will have to "read" the pitch. When facing a power pitcher, you might want to stand deeper in the box; this will allow you a longer look at the ball. If you are facing a breaking-ball or sinker-ball pitcher, you might want to move up in the box; you will have a better chance to hit the pitch before it breaks. But remember: If you move up, you are closer to the pitcher and that gives you less time to react to a fast ball.

If you consider yourself a pull hitter, you will move closer to the plate. Hitters with slow bat speed might be more successful further back in the box. You alone must determine where to stand, considering that your position can be adjusted according to the type of pitcher throwing.

Your feet should be a little more than shoulder-width apart. (Driving the ball becomes difficult if the feet are *too* far apart.) In addition, too wide a stance will restrict the hips and slow you down when you are leaving the box. If your feet are too close together, it could result in lunging at the ball; an ideal stance is one which is somewhere in between and is comfortable for you. Your weight should be on the front halves of your feet.

Many young hitters tend to have the back shoulder lower than the front. This forces the hitter to upper-cut the ball and makes the swing long and slow. *The front shoulder should be level with, or slightly lower than the back shoulder.* This will help you swing down on the ball. A *slight* bend at the waist and knees will help you relax as you wait for the pitch. Your hands should be about chest-high and about 6" away from the point of your back shoulder (directly out from the back arm pit). *The further away from the body your hands are, the more you will sweep the bat— sweeping will result in loss of speed and control of the bat.* If you have your hands too close to your body, you will drag the bat (or "inside-out" your swing), and will probably hit a lot of balls to the opposite field. In addition, dragging the bat reduces bat speed.

These are the three basic bat stances:

1. OPEN STANCE: Your front foot should be further from home-plate than your back foot. This stance is helpful to players who are having trouble picking up the breaking ball. If you use this stance, it is important that you *step toward the pitcher,* otherwise you may have some trouble with the outside pitch.

2. THE STRAIGHTAWAY STANCE: Both feet are about the same distance away from the plate. You *must step toward the pitcher.*

3. THE CLOSED STANCE: The front foot is closer to the plate than the back foot. This is probably used more often than any other stance. The closed stance helps you to keep your head and shoulders in and enables you to stay with the breaking ball a little longer. When you use this stance, you might want to get off the plate a little more and stride toward the pitcher, (being careful not to lock your hips.) This stance aids in driving the ball to the opposite field.

HITTING SUMMARY

As you have learned, there is a lot more to hitting than just swing-ing the bat. Each batter must take advantage of his individual abilities, must find a style of hitting which is suited for him, and must develop a positive mental attitude which will enable him to handle the pressure of hitting in various game situations. Once he has done this, he will be a successful hitter, and will have the con-fidence it takes to do his job right. *Remember:* "Success breeds confidence and confidence breeds success."

Courage and Concentration are two elements which, more than anything else, can determine the success or failure of a hitter. Without courage, there is no way a hitter can achieve concentration. With the ball traveling at speeds in excess of 80 MPH, it takes courage for a hitter to concentrate on hitting the ball while disregarding the possibility that he may strike out, or he may not get the sacrifice his team so badly needs or—worst of all—that he may be hit by the pitch. *It takes courage to concentrate.* Further, as a player advances in classification, he is exposed to more and more outside interference. There are more fans, bigger ballparks, and a lot more distractions. Without *total* concentration, the hitter will not be able to perform at his optimum level. *A successful hitter can block out everything except the ball as it leaves the pitcher's hand.*

HITTING TIPS

1. *Select a bat you can handle.*

2. *Keep your head still—back and down with the pitch (following the ball into the catcher's mitt).*

3. *Direct your entire attention to the ball.*

4. *Hit strikes.*

5. *Keep front shoulder and chin tucked in.*

6. *Swing fungo for bat speed.*

7. *Don't commit too soon.*

8. *Hit the ball where it's pitched. Learn to hit to all fields.*

9. *Turn your head so both eyes are on the pitcher—don't look around your nose.*

10 *Lay the bat on your shoulder while waiting for the pitcher to get ready.*

11. *If you hold the bat up for any length of time—this will cause tension in your hands and arms and detracts from a free and fluid swing. In addition, you may "loop" the bat.*

12. *Hit your strength. Every hitter has a strength, just as every pitcher has a weakness. Wait for your pitch.*

13. *Stay on the balls of your feet.*

14. *Keep off your heels.*

15. *Be ready to hit. Get the bat off your shoulder before the pitcher delivers the ball.*

16. *When stepping in to hit, make sure you have maximum plate coverage.*

17. *Get a comfortable stance in the batter's box.*

18. *Look to see where the fat part of the bat is in covering home plate. Don't have your handle over the plate.*

19. *Start the bat to create hand action and bat speed; if you like the pitch, hit it—if you don't, hold up your swing.*

20. *Stride into the pitch.*

21. *Swing down on all pitches to create a level swing.*

22. *Keep your stride short.*

23. *Don't overswing.*

24. *Look for the fast ball. Adjust to the off-speed pitch.*

25. *Make the pitcher come to you—don't go out after him.*

26. *Keep your hands back and hit with your hands, not your head.*

27. *Keep your hands relaxed; as contact is made, your hands will tighten.*

28. *When hitting to the opposite field, hit the ball on the ground. You do this by hitting down on the ball.*

29. *Faster ballplayers should take advantage of their speed—concentrate on hitting the ball on the ground and making contact.*

30. *Choke up if you are having trouble controlling the bat. With two strikes, choking up will give you better bat control.*

31. *Don't fall away at home plate—keep your buttocks in.*

32. *Be aggressive with the bat.*

33. *Follow through with your swing after contact is made—don't quit your swing.*

34. *Hit with your top hand and roll your wrist after contact.*

35. *Don't let the barrel of the bat get ahead of your hands too soon.*

HITTING PROBLEMS AND SOLUTIONS

PROBLEM: Overstriding

SOLUTIONS:

1. You can shorten your stride by widening your stance.

2. Put exaggerated weight on your back leg.

3. Bend your knees and crouch, shifting your weight to the ball of your back foot.

PROBLEM: Sweeping the bat

SOLUTIONS:
1. The bat should be in the fingers, not far back in the hand.

2. Relax your arms and roll your wrist after contact.

3. Try to achieve a sensation of hitting only with your wrist.

4. "Feel" the bat in your hands. Start hands forward *toward the pitcher* (not out and forward).

PROBLEM: Hand Hitches (The hitter constantly gets hit on the fist or has trouble getting the bat back up and through in time to hit the pitch.)

SOLUTIONS:
1. Move your hands back instead of dropping them down.

2. Put your bat on your shoulder. Bring your hands up until they are parallel with the shoulders and hit from there. *Do not pick the bat up. Just hit from the shoulder.*

PROBLEM: Head Pulling

SOLUTIONS:

1. Don't look where the ball will go.

2. Watch the ball hit the bat and hit the ball up the middle.

3. Don't try to pull the ball.

4. Swing down. In taking a longer look to swing down, your head will automatically have to look at the ball longer.

5. Don't try to hit the ball in the air.

6. Keep your chin and shoulders tucked in and keep your head steady.

PROBLEM: Uppercutting

SOLUTIONS:

1. Carry your bat flat, not vertical.

2. Lay your bat on your shoulder and don't pick it up until the pitcher is ready to throw.

3. *Concentrate* on swinging down on the ball. Though you can't actually swing down, the down arc will force you to swing level.

4. Practice hitting the ball on the ground.

5. Keep your shoulders and hips level and *don't drop your back shoulder to hit.*

HITTING EXERCISES

WRISTS AND FOREARMS:

Do wrist curls, using a 5 lb. dumbbell. Hold the dumbbell with your palm up. Using only the wrist, raise and lower the weight until you feel a burning sensation. Now, turn the palm down and repeat.

Do the same exercise again, rotating the wrist from side to side this time. Do this every other day. When you can do 100 reps without burning, increase the weight to 10 lbs.

BAT SPEED:

Using a batting tee, swing a bat at least 100 times. If no batting tee is available, a small homemade "ball" (use rags, as paper will tear) hanging from a string works just as well. A broom handle can be used in place of a bat. This is an excellent drill for improving hand-eye coordination. Swinging a weighted bat is also an excellent way to increase your bat speed.

SLUMPS

No book on baseball would be complete without a section on "slumps". Slumps are to a ballplayer what bunyons are to a mailman—they're painful, they're irritating, and every ballplayer is going to have one sooner or later. What most ballplayers don't realize is that slumps usually begin when the hitter is doing *well* at the plate. A hitter builds a "hot streak" over a period of time. Likewise, he "cools off" over a period of time. All some players need is *one* bad game or *one* poor at-bat and they begin to doubt their hitting ability. They begin to ask themselves what they're doing wrong. They often begin to overswing in an effort to compensate; they may change their stance or adjust their hands. Maybe they'll "tighten up" or wear the same sox they wore the last time they had a base hit. In short, a player who feels he's in a slump will do virtually *anything* to get on base. Though he may only be 0-for-10, he feels like he's 0-for-100; thus is born "The Slump".

Though slumps are sometimes the result of doing something mechanically wrong, they are more often caused by the hitter's mental attitude. he begins to doubt his ability, and instead of approaching the plate with a positive mental attitude and a feeling of confidence, he goes up to bat subconsciously thinking that he *won't* hit the ball. Slumps which result from a poor mental attitude are much harder to deal with. The most common complaint from hitters who feel they are in a slump is that they "just aren't seeing the ball". If the hitter isn't seeing the ball, he's not *concentrating on the ball.* He's probably thinking about his mechanics, his statistics, or perhaps a defensive misque he committed in the previous inning. Oftentimes, the player approaches the plate thinking "I've *got* to get a hit", when he should be thinking *"watch the ball".*

Visualization is a useful tool in dealing with the problem of not seeing the ball. Visualization is a mental technique whereby one *imagines* himself in a certain hitting (or, in the case of pitchers, a pitching) situation. Visualization enables the player to mentally "replay" a situation where he struck out, or chased a bad pitch. For example: When a player swings at, and misses a pitch he usually hits, he can remove himself from the batter's box and quickly replay the pitch again, this time *visualizing the results he wants.*

Great hitters like Carl Yazstremski and Willie Stargell admit to taking "mental BP" before every game; they consider it an important part of their pre-game preparation. Like good hitting, visualization is a *skill,* and must be *practiced.* The more realistic the visualization, the more beneficial it will be. Developing strong mental images may require standing in the proper stance, with a bat in your hand. If this is what it takes for you to get a *clear mental image,* then by all means, do it. In a good visualization, the hitter will *see* the ball as it leaves the pitcher's hand. (You should go so far as to know exactly who the pitcher is...) He will *feel* the ball hit the bat and he will *hear* how it sounds. Imagine what happens *after* a hit—see yourself rounding the bases; hear the cheers of the crowd...

This type of *positive visualization* can and should be practiced daily. The more the player carries positive mental images in his mind, the more successful he will be. It takes practice. It requires concentration. *It works!*

TO SUMMARIZE

1. *Concentrate on "seeing" the ball.*

2. *Don't rush yourself.*

3. *Be mentally ready before you step into the batter's box.*

4. *Check your mechanics.*

5. *Be emotionally in control before you enter the batter's box. Learn to control your breathing and relax. Concentrate on positive visualizations.*

6. *Consider only two things while you are in the box: 1) Are you comfortable? and 2) Do you see the ball?*

7. *Don't experiment in batting practice in an effort to find a solution for your problem at the plate. This can be harmful;*

47

you may develop bad habits which will carry over to actual game situations. Use BP to stay lose and keep your fundamentals sharp. If you concentrate and relax, your "problem" will take care of itself.

5

BUNTING

Bunting is one of the most important plays in baseball. Unfortunately, it is also one of the most poorly executed. Failure to advance a baserunner is probably the primary reason for losing ballgames. A hitter who can lay down a bunt when necessary increases his value a thousandfold. *Practice bunting on a regular basis.*

There are three basic types of bunts: 1) The sacrifice bunt, 2) the drag, or push bunt, and 3) the suicide squeeze.

THE SACRIFICE BUNT:

When attempting a sacrifice bunt, the batter must "sacrifice" his turn at bat to advance the runner. He does this by placing the ball on the *ground, in a good location.* He is *not trying to get a base hit.* If the batter tries to be too perfect, waits too long to show the bunt, or runs before the ball is on the ground, he often indicates that he is trying to reach base safely.

SQUARING TO BUNT:

There are two methods used when squaring to bunt.

1. Squaring Around: The back foot is moved forward so the toes are parallel to each other.

2. Heel-Toe Pivot: The hitter pivots on the heel of his front foot and the toe of his back foot. This type of pivot can be used in all three bunting situations. It allows the hitter to wait a little longer and does not tip off the opposing team that you are bunting.

With either method, it is important that the hips and shoulders be square to the pitcher. *Do not try to be too perfect in the placement of the bunted ball.* You should be thinking. "If I bunt the ball, it will be close to the line (usually toward 1st), not too hard. If

49

I miss it, it will go foul and I'll have another chance..." *Never hit the ball back to the pitcher.*

BUNTING WITH RUNNERS AT 1ST AND 2ND:

The best place to sacrifice in this situation is down the 3rd base line. You want the 3rd baseman to field the ball. The bunt should be close to the line so the pitcher can't get it, and *hard* enough so the 3rd baseman must charge. (Usually, the 1st baseman will be charging hard; this is the reason for bunting toward 3rd.)

Once the bunt sign has been given, the hitter should move up in the batter's box, toward the pitcher. This gives him a better chance of keeping the ball in fair territory after it is bunted. The further back the hitter stands in the box, the greater chance he has of hitting the ball foul. Obviously, too drastic a change in the batter's position will alert the opposition that a bunt play is on. Once the hitter has squared his hips and shoulders toward the pitcher, he should:

1. Bend slightly at the knees.

2. Shift most of his weight to his front foot. This will keep him from lunging at the ball.

3. *Slide* his top hand up the barrel of the bat, approximately to the trademark area. The bat should be held with the fingers in a pinch-type grasp—this will keep the fingers from being hit by the ball.

4. Extending both arms forward, keep the top hand at the top of your strike zone. The bottom hand should be about 1" lower. The bat should stay at this level. If you flatten it, any ball in the air will probably be caught. With the bat held at the proper angle, most balls hit in the air will go foul.

5. The hitter should bend at the knees, *keeping his eyes on the same plain as the ball.*

6. *Don't "jab" at the ball.* Try to "catch" it on the barrel of the bat. Be careful not to grip the bat too tightly.

7. *Bunt the ball on the bottom half of the bat.* Keeping the bat at the proper angle will help you do this.

8. The bottom hand guides the angle of the bat. For example, a righthanded hitter, sacrificing to 1st, would point the nob of his bat toward 3rd. If he was buntining to 3rd, he would point

the barrel toward 1st.

9. Arms should be slightly bent and out away from the body.

10. *Bunt strikes when possible.* Don't try to bunt the high fastball; it is the most difficult pitch to bunt. *Think down*—the ball must be belt-high or lower.

BUNTING FOR A BASE HIT:

Learn to recognize the defense: Which men are playing "in" and which are playing "back"? When the 3rd baseman is even with the bag, he is playing in. The righthanded hitter can assume that anytime the 3rd baseman is even with the bag or deeper, he is back far enough for a successful bunt. For lefthanded hitters, if you learn to bunt properly, you can beat the ball even if the 3rd baseman is on the edge of the grass. *You must practice!*

Practice until you can bunt 5 out of 10 times successfully. A good bunter becomes a real threat because he forces the 1st, 2nd and 3rd basemen to play in—this increases his chance of putting a ball through the infield hole for a base hit.

In addition, a consistently good bunter intimidates pitchers.

THE DRAG BUNT:

A good drag bunter can increase his batting average by as much as 20 points. *Proper execution* and *Deception* are the keys to a successful drag bunt. It is not necessary for a drag bunter to be exceptionally fast; *when and where* the ball is bunted will determine how successful he is.

Most drag bunt attempts occur on the first pitch. If no attempt is made, many coaches have the corner men drop back. If you are a confident bunter, the best time to bunt is after the first pitch.

RIGHTHANDED DRAG BUNT:

1. Cheat *up* in the batter's box slightly.

2. Move the right foot back slightly away from the plate as the ball is released.

3. *Slide* the right hand up to the trademark area, gripping the bat the same way you would for a sacrifice bunt. The left hand pulls the knob down to a position approximately six inches in

front of the right hip. *Keep the barrel of the bat slightly up.*

4. *Always look for the perfect bunt.* You want to bunt the ball just fair, or in foul territory but *never back to the pitcher.*

5. *Bunt strikes*—look for a ball *down.*

6. Don't run too soon.

7. Hands and arms should be out in front. Don't let the ball penetrate the strike zone too far. This will cause you to bunt the ball back to the pitcher.

LEFTHANDED DRAG BUNT:

1. Cheat *up* in the box.

2. Open your front foot slightly.

3. Shift your weight to the right foot as the ball leaves the pitcher's hand. The left foot comes forward (cross-over step) *directly toward the pitcher.*

4. *Never attempt to run before the ball has made contact with the bat.*

5. The right hand is the guide; you can drag down the 1st or 3rd base line.

6. The left hand should slide up the barrel in the same manner as for a sacrifice bunt.

7. *Bunt Strikes.*

8. Don't attempt to bunt the high fast ball.

9. The ball should be just fair, or foul giving you another chance.

10. The barrel of the bat should be slightly up.

11. Bunt the ball on the bottom half of the bat and keep it out of the air.

52

12. Don't grip the bat too tightly; you want to deaden the ball.

THE PUSH BUNT:

The push bunt is used when the 1st baseman is playing back. The ideal time to attempt a push bunt is when you have a lefthanded pitcher who falls off the side of the mound, is a poor fielder, or is slow covering 1st base.

The ball is "pushed" on the ground somewhere between the pitcher and the 1st baseman. The ball must be hit softly enough so that the 2nd baseman can't handle it; the ideal spot is on the grass, just before the dirt.

The perfect time for a push bunt is when you have a weak hitter at the plate, the tying or winning run at 2nd and *no outs.* You *must advance the runner to 3rd* in this situation. You may have already failed a sacrifice bunt attempt and you cannot afford a ground ball to the left side of the infield, stranding the runner at 2nd.

The push bunt is used primarily by righthanded hitters because placement of the ball is so important. A lefthanded hitter can pull the ball on the ground using the same techniques as on the drag bunt, but the ball must be hit a little harder. *The ball must get past the pitcher in order for the bunt to be successful.*

RIGHTHANDED HITTER PUSH BUNT:

1. The ball should be up, preferably a fast ball, and out over the plate.

2. After the ball is released, the hitter should move his right hand up toward the trademark, just as he would in the other bunts. He will hold the bat a little firmer with his right hand. He is not trying to deaden the ball, just push it past the pitcher.

3. The barrel of the bat should be slightly up.

4. *Don't* extend your arms.

5. Bring the nob of the bat close to the left side of your chest. Your right hand should be at the top of your strike zone.

6. Weight should shift to the left side, exactly as in the heel-toe pivot in the sacrifice bunt. This is done as the ball is

released; the right foot starts forward on contact.

7. Hands and arms should push the bat to the ball, pushing the ball *on the ground between the pitcher and 1st baseman.*

8. Hit strikes up in the strike zone.

9. *Practice! Practice! Practice!*

SUICIDE SQUEEZE:

The suicide squeeze is an offensive weapon usually used late in the game. The batter attempts to bunt in the tying or winning run, which is on 3rd base.

Billy Martin used the squeeze very effectively. By having a reputation for using the squeeze, many managers would try to outsmart Billy by pitching out. If they guessed wrong, the pitcher would be in the hole and eventually, would have to throw a strike.

The squeeze is usually used when the batter is ahead of the pitcher on the count.

TIPS FOR EXECUTING THE SQUEEZE:

1. As soon as the "squeeze" sign is given, the batter *must bunt the next pitch,* no matter where the ball is thrown.

2. The ball must be hit *on the ground.*

3. It doesn't have to be a perfect bunt.

4. Don't reveal your strategy by squaring too soon. In higher classifications of baseball, the pitcher is instructed to knock the hitter down if he squares too soon.

5. Don't run before the ball has made contact with the bat. *You are not bunting for a base hit.*

6. Use whatever bunting method you have the most success with.

7. *The runner at 3rd must not break too soon.** If he does, the pitcher can throw a pitch which the batter has no chance to bunt. For example, in the Major Leagues, if the runner breaks too soon and the pitcher has time to adjust, he'll throw the ball at the batter's neck. I can tell you from experience: "That's a tough ball to bunt!"

*Leading off is not permitted in Little League.

The runner at 3rd should take his normal lead. When the pitcher starts his wind up, the baserunner should start *walking* toward home. When the pitcher's front foot hits the ground, the runner should *break hard* for home. If the batter misses the ball, try and keep from being tagged out until the other baserunners advance to scoring position.

6

BASERUNNING

Numerous games are won or lost on the basepaths. The importance of good baserunning cannot be overstressed. Baserunning should be diligently practiced.

Below is a list of things a good baserunner should know:

The signs.

The game situation: outs, score, inning, etc.

Always force the fielders to hurry—this can cause a situation for an error.

Always challenge an outfielder on balls hit to his glove hand.

Be daring and aggressive, but never foolish.

All baserunning is controlled by the game situation.

Know the pitcher's weaknesses.

Run through the 1st bag.

Know your own speed and the condition of the infield.

Know the strength of the outfielder's arm. You can be more aggressive with a righthanded right fielder, as his momentum will carry him away from any possible throw to the infield. Likewise with the lefthanded left fielder.

Good judgment is the key to good baserunning.

TAKING LEADS* AND STEALING BASES:

Always take your lead anticipating the catcher's best throw. After the pitch makes contact with the catcher's glove, the baserunner's first few steps should be hard back to the bag.

THE PRIMARY LEAD:

The runner takes a primary lead when the pitcher is in the set position. His *main concern is his ability to get back to 1st base*. The length of his lead is determined by:

1. His ability to get back to 1st.

2. The game situation.

3. The condition of the infield.

If the steal sign is on, the runner will use one of the following primary leads:

1. The Two-Way Lead: The runner wants to be as far away from 1st as possible, but must be close enough to get back safely if the pitcher attempts to pick him off. The runner's right foot should be a little behind the left and slightly open toward 2nd. This will give him quicker acceleration toward 2nd base. Baserunners should remain relaxed while in their stealing stance; if the pitcher holds the ball too long, it's up to the hitter to protect the runner by calling for a time-out. If the runner remains too long in his stealing stance he will stiffen up, making it difficult for him to get his best jump toward 2nd base. The runner begins his acceleration toward 2nd as soon as he knows that the pitcher is going to deliver to the plate.

2. The One-Way Lead: The primary objective of the one-way lead is for the baserunner to force the pitcher to try and pick him off. With a one-way lead, you are *not attempting to steal*, you are just helping the 1st base coach and the rest of the team pick up a "key" in the pitcher's move which will aid other runners in getting a better jump. Take a larger lead than normal. On the pitcher's first movement, you must break back to the 1st base bag. If he throws home, you must recover and get into your secondary lead.

THE SECONDARY LEAD:

The runner moves from the primary into the secondary lead by taking 3 short shuffle steps toward 2nd base *after the pitcher releases the ball*. The runner should watch the ball leave the pitcher's hand.

*Leading off is not permitted in Little League.

Again, his lead should be as large as possible while still enabling him to return safely to 1st in the event of a pick-off attempt. This distance varies with each runner and must be perfected during practice sessions. The 1st base coach will watch the pitcher and advise the runner if the pitcher makes a move toward 1st. The length of the secondary lead is determined by:

1. The length of the primary lead the runner has taken.

2. The runner's speed.

3. The catcher's arm.

4. The condition of the infield.

5. The position of the 1st baseman.

6. The pitcher—right or lefthanded?

7. Does the score of the game allow the runner to take a chance?

THE WALKING LEAD:

After the pitcher begins to go into his set position, the runner takes short, controlled side steps toward 2nd base. This allows him to be in motion when he takes off for 2nd. All good pitchers will force the baseruner to stop; use caution so you can get back to the bag. This lead is usually used by baserunners who don't normally steal.

THE FALSE BREAK:

The runner takes several quick steps toward 2nd, stops and checks to see where the ball is. This breaks up the infield as it causes the SS or 2nd baseman to shift their positions,* depending upon who is covering the bag on a steal. The baserunner puts pressure on the defense and often on the pitcher as he hurrys his throw to homeplate.

*If done properly, the 1st baseman will yell "There he goes!"

THE DELAYED STEAL:

If the baserunner feels that the SS, 2nd baseman and catcher are not alert, he will take his normal lead, making his usual move toward 2nd base. He will use three side steps; at the end of the third step, he will break hard for 2nd base. The baserunner who utilizes this technique is normally not a basestealing threat.

THE DOUBLE STEAL—1ST AND 3RD SITUATION:

The runner going into 2nd lays back as the infielder attempts to tag him, putting himself in a run-down situation so the runner at 3rd can score. If the infielder throws to home, the runner continues on to 2nd base.

Knowing that the double steal is in order, the runner on 3rd walks directly on the 3rd base foul line. If he stays in front of the bag, the catcher will not be able to determine the length of his lead. When the runner has an extended, safe lead, he will stop and watch the pitcher's delivery to home plate. At this point, the runner on 1st breaks for 2nd. When the runner at 3rd sees the catcher's throw go over the pitcher's head to 2nd base, he breaks for home.

Watch for a fake throw to 2nd. Be sure you see the throw go over the pitcher's head!

The runner at 1st must watch the runner at 2nd. The runner at 2nd must use a sign to alert the runner at 1st that he is going. *The runner at 1st must break with the runner at 2nd, thus eliminating a 1st and 3rd situation and a possible double play.* If the runner at 1st does not break and the runner at 2nd gets thrown out at 3rd, you won't have a runner in scoring position.

THE STRAIGHT STEAL:

With the steal sign on, the runner wants to get as big a lead as possible (see "Leads"). Once the lead has been established, the baserunner will look for some flaw in the pitcher's delivery that will help him to get the maximum jump. Remember: Bases are stolen as a result of the pitcher's weakness. Below are some "keys" to look for that will aid you in finding these weaknesses.

RIGHTHANDED PITCHERS:

Look for:

1. Opening of the front shoulder.

2. Cracking of the front knee.

3. Does he lean away from home plate?

4. Is there movement of his back right heel?

5. Is his movement exaggerated, either quick or slow?

LEFTHANDED PITCHERS:

Look for:

1. Is he leaning back?

2. Does he lean toward, or away from home plate?

3. Where does he look on his first movement?

4. Is his leg straight?

5. Is his movement exaggerated, either quick or slow?

*When stealing 3rd, remember that most lefties break or bend the back leg before throwing home.

Once a potential basestealer has picked up a "key" and gotten the maximum lead, I suggest that the right foot be a little behind the left and opened slightly toward 2nd base. Weight should be on the balls of your feet, hands should *not* be on your knees.

Your first move is to pivot on the ball of your right foot, dropping the right arm and shoulder toward 2nd base as you cross over with your left foot. Stay low, driving off toward 2nd.

There are two different theories regarding position of the head when stealing a base. One is that the baserunner should take a quick peek into the home plate area to pick up the action; the other is that the runner should lower his head and concentrate on only one thing— beating the ball to the bag. The method you choose is purely a matter of personal preference.

THE THREE MOST COMMON
BASERUNNING SITUATIONS:

1. Runner on 1st—no outs: Do not get thrown out at 3rd on a base hit. You are in a much better situation with runners at 1st and 2nd and no outs than you are with one out and a runner on 1st.

2. Runner on 1st—1 out: This is a good time to take a chance and try to go from 1st to 3rd if you think you can make it. With runners at both corners, you can get a run on a squeeze, a sacrifice fly or a missed double play.

3. Runner on 1st—2 outs: Don't get thrown out at 3rd on a base

hit. Any runner who can get from 1st to 3rd on a sharp base hit can score from 2nd on the same. The squeeze, sacrifice fly, or a missed double play do not exist with two outs; the passed ball or error are often few and far between.

HIT AND RUN SITUATION:

Remember, in a hit and run situation, *you are not attempting to steal a base* so you might want to shorten your lead. *make sure the pitcher is throwing to home plate before you break.*

Break on the pitch, with a quick peek into the home plate area to pick up the action. If you can't find the ball, look for help from the 3rd base coach.

Don't be fooled by the infielder's reactions.

If a line drive is hit, just keep going; you couldn't get back anyway.

ROUNDING THE BASES:

Ideally, the baserunner wants to take as short a turn as possible without losing speed on his approach to the bag. As speed and running style vary with each individual runner, each should be encouraged and coached in developing a base-rounding technique which is most suitable for him. Once the runner or the 1st base coach has established that a turn at 1st base is necessary, the runner's concentration should be devoted to that *one* thing: *Rounding the bases.*

GENERAL INSTRUCTIONS FOR ROUNDING BASES:

Concentrate

Touch Every Base

Push Off The Front Inside Corner Of The Bag*

Dip Left Shoulder And Don't Break Your Stride

*It is preferable to use the left foot; this helps the runer get a good lean and enables him to push toward 2nd with his right foot.

ROUNDING 1st:

1. Begin to veer out (approximately 3') as soon as you leave the

batter's box. The key is for each individual to find the perfect spot on the basepath to begin his turn.

2. Approach the bag just outside of the foul line (about 7') and further out if necessary.

3. Glance quickly at the bag as you touch it. Your body should lean toward the infield side of 1st base on contact with the bag; this makes it easier to push off toward 2nd. As soon as you have touched the bag...

4. Locate the ball.

5. Round the bag aggressively, generating speed toward 2nd base. Make the outfielder hurry—this may cause him to misplay the ball. *Make the outfielder stop you.* (Sometimes, this maneuver can cause an inexperienced outfielder to throw to 1st—if this happens, you should be on your way to 2nd base.)

ROUNDING 2ND:

When the runner is about 30' from the bag he should pick up the 3rd base coach on balls hit behind him.

ROUNDING 3RD:

The runner is guided by hand signs from the 3rd base coach. Run *hard* and *do only what the 3rd base coach tells you;* the outfielder or relay man may misplay the ball.

SIGNS FROM THE 3RD BASE COACH:

SIGN	MEANS
Waves one or both arms in the air in a circular motion:	Score on the play.
Holds both arms high in the air:	Do not attempt to score.
On one knee, bringing both arms down toward the ground:	A play will be made at 3rd base and the runner must *slide* into the bag.

As soon as the runner rounds the bag, he should locate the ball. If the ball has been mishandled, valuable time would be lost if the runner relied on the coach for this information.

62

RUNNING TO 1ST BASE:

A good follow through enables the hitter to get out of the batter's box quickly. The lefthanded hitter has an obvious advantage when leaving the box; his follow through automatically carries him toward 1st base. By contrast, the righthanded hitter carries his body away from 1st base on his follow through; he is forced to push off with his left foot and shift his weight in the direction of the base. He may lose as many as two or three steps in doing this.

THINGS TO REMEMBER WHEN RUNNING TO 1ST:

Don't look to where the ball was hit.

Concentrate only on building up your speed toward 1st base.

Stay low the first few steps, then get into proper running form: Propel yourself with your arms and upper body. (See: "Power Running")

Pick up the ball through the corner of your eye.

Run slightly to the outside of the 1st base foul line—this is done so that if the pitcher or catcher throws to 1st and hits you, you won't be called out for obstruction.

Run in a straight line, keeping eyes focused on the front of the bag.

Run full speed through the bag.

Never jump or leap into the bag.

Lean across the bag on contact—don't lunge or break your stride.

Run full speed to 1st on every play.

After touching the bag, look to foul territory for a wild throw.

Watch the 1st baseman's feet.* If he moves down the 1st base line, you may have to slide into 1st to avoid a tag. This is the only time you slide into 1st base!!

*This is a very difficult maneuver and is a purely instinctive play. Very seldom do you have time to think about sliding. If this play is not properly executed, injury may occur.

AFTER YOU REACH 1ST BASE:

1. Review the game situation: Number of outs, score, inning, hitter at the plate, etc.

2. Keep your left foot on the bag.

3. Check the position of the outfielders and know the strength of their arms.

4. Check the 3rd base coach for a sign.

5. Take your lead toward 2nd. From 2½ to 4½ steps (this represents the full length of your body). *Never cross over when taking your lead.* Steps should be short, sliding side-steps. Keep your hands off your knees.

6. After you have taken your lead, weight should be on the balls of your feet, knees bent, heels off the ground, arms relaxed in front of your body, eyes focused on the pitcher.

7. When going *back* to 1st, touch the far corner of the bag with the left foot, swinging the body to the right and planting your right foot in foul territory somewhere in the direction of right field. *Always check the 1st base coach as you return to the bag.* Or, slide in head-first, touching the outside corner of the bag with your right hand. This is *not a leap;* stay low to the ground and drive with your legs. By touching the outside of the bag, you lengthen the tag for the 1st baseman. Always turn your head away from the ball.

8. Never take your eyes off the ball.

9. Know the pitcher and his weakness.

THE RUNNER AT 2ND BASE:

1. Always approach 2nd with the intention of going to 3rd, but *watch the 3rd base coach*—he'll tell you whether or not to continue on to 3rd.

2. Be prepared to slide if there is a chance for a force play.

3. The runner at 2nd can usually take a bigger lead than the runner at 1st *if* he feels it's necessary. The ideal lead from 2nd base is 5 or 6 steps. As the pitcher commits to home plate, the runner may slide into a 20-25' lead.

4. Take your lead slightly behind the straight line from 2nd to 3rd. This allows a good turning radius around 3rd.

5. Be conscious of the SS—he may step in behind the runner for a pickoff.

THE RUNNER AT 3RD BASE:

1. With 1 or no outs, shorten your lead so you can't get picked off on a line drive.

2. Always take your lead in foul territory; this will eliminate the possibility of you getting called out if you are hit by the ball.

3. The length of your lead is determined by: The distance the 3rd baseman has from the bag, whether or not the 3rd base coach wants you to go on any ground ball, and the strength of the catcher's arm.

4. As soon as the ball crosses the plate you want to get on the infield side of the line in order to obstruct the throw from the catcher to the 3rd baseman.

5. Never commit to home plate until you are certain that the pitcher is going to deliver to the hitter.

6. With a righthanded hitter at the plate, the runner at 3rd can add a step to his secondary lead. This is possible because the hitter obstructs the catcher's view of the runner.

7. Be alert for wild pitches and passed balls. The coach cannot help you here—it's up to you whether to go or not.

8. Hips and shoulders should be pointed toward home plate. Right foot in the air and heading toward the ground as the ball reaches the hitting zone. If the batter does not swing at the pitch, the baserunner immediately pivots on the balls of his feet, drives off his right foot and breaks hard back to the bag *in fair territory.*

SLIDING:

Sliding is probably the most difficult fundamental that a ballplayer must learn. If not done properly, serious injury may result. The younger player's anxiety over getting hurt sometimes makes sliding a difficult thing to teach. The coach's patience and understanding are vitally important.

The baserunner usually slides for three reasons: 1) to get to the bag, 2) to avoid a tag, or 3) to break up a double play.

THE BENT-LEG OR "STRAIGHT" SLIDE:

1. Begin the slide approximately 10' from the bag.

2. Don't slide too close to the bag.

3. Take off from either leg and bend it under.

4. Keep the weight on the outside of the bent leg. The calf should break the slide, followed by the thigh and then the rear-end.

5. *Don't leap or jump into the slide.*

6. Stay low to the ground.

7. As both legs bend, throw your head slightly backward. This prevents the knees from hitting the ground.

8. Always touch the base with the toe of the foot that is extended.

9. Keep the leg relaxed, knee slightly bent and the *heel off the ground.*

THE HOOK SLIDE:

The hook slide can be made to either side of the bag and is used to avoid a tag. The runner slides to the side *opposite* where the infielder has indicated he will catch the ball. The hook slide is used when the baserunner feels that the ball will beat him to the bag.

The hook slide is slower than the straight slide because the runner is forced to tag the base with the leg farthest back. For example, if the runner is sliding to the right side of the bag he will tag the base with his left foot.

When sliding to the right side (most common), the runner will push off the left foot just before starting his slide.

1. Feet and legs should be extended in front of the body. Legs *should not* be tucked.

2. The runner slides more on the upper thigh than on the calf

and leg.

3. The runner should not bend the left knee any more than necessary to touch the base. The more the knee bends, the longer it will take to touch the base.

BREAKING UP THE DOUBLE PLAY:*

This type of slide increases the chance of injury as the baserunner attempts to make contact with the pivot man at 2nd base. Either the bent-leg or the hook slide may be used.

The purpose of this slide is to disrupt the infielder's pivot and his throw to another base. In addition, the anticipation of a hard slide threatens an infielder and may keep him from trying the same movement if a similar situation arises.

Remember: you are *not* trying to hurt the pivot man. You're only attempting to disrupt his concentration and his throw to 1st base.

1. During infield, watch which side of the bag the SS and 2nd baseman make their pivot and throw. This will enable you to slide to that point before the pivot man gets there.

2. You should attempt to disrupt the infielder by driving into his lower legs, knocking his legs out from under him. Use the upper part of your foot (shoe-string area) *not your cleats*, to make the contact with the pivot man's leg.

3. When you slide, you must be able to make contact with the base with some part of your body. If you can't, you will be called out and so will the runner going to 1st.

4. *Don't use a rolling block.* Not only is this dangerous for the slider and the infielder, it is *illegal* and you will be called out. The slider must be on the ground when he makes contact with the infielder.

SLIDING HEAD-FIRST:

Avoid sliding head-first whenever possible. Many injuries are

*This information is included for the benefit of higher classifications of baseball. Please be advised that Little League Baseball does not encourage a specific type of play intended to break up a double play.

caused as a result of head-first sliding. A runner can break a finger, jam a shoulder, suffer neck injuries. With his fingers exposed on the bag, it is easy for an infielder to step on them, causing serious problems.

Never slide head-first into home plate!! The catcher can drop his shin guards in your face. The area around home plate is very hard and often has holes where the hitters have dug in; a baserunner can jam a finger, or suffer serious injury to his neck or shoulders.

SUMMARY

1. *When in doubt, slide!*

2. *Concentrate on the base you are sliding into.*

3. *Keep your hands and arms above your head.*

4. *Don't run over the catcher if you can avoid it; you run over the catcher only if he completely takes the line and home plate away from you. If you can see any sign of home plate, slide for it! If a collision with the catcher is unavoidable, hit him on his glove side; you may knock the ball out of his hand. Stay low!*

PLAYING THE POSITIONS

PITCHING

Obviously, pitching is the best defense a team can have. As with hitting, pitching is an individual thing and depends upon several factors, physical strength and mental composition foremost among them. There are no hard and fast rules when it comes to pitching but there are some specifics which all young pitchers should be aware of.

First of all, the pitcher must recognize his capabilities. In the case of Little Leaguers, this is the responsibility of the parents and the coach. In my opinion, many young pitchers make a mistake by trying to throw a curve ball before they are ready. Their arms aren't strong enough at an early age and further, there are very few amateur coaches qualified to instruct a young athlete in the proper way to throw a breaking pitch. My advice to all beginning pitchers is: *Learn how to throw a fast ball. Throw it hard and throw it for strikes.*

Ideally, every pitcher should have three good pitches. He should strive to perfect these three pitches before he even thinks about trying to develop a fourth. *Young pitchers should strive for control.* Find a target and throw to it! Catfish Hunter once told me that he used to spend hours just throwing baseballs through an old tire which swung from a tree in his back yard. *It doesn't matter how hard a pitcher throws if he can't put the ball where he wants it.*

I would guess that 100% of the successful pitchers in the Major Leagues would tell you that their preparation for a game begins days before they actually step onto the mound. Tom Seaver once said that "Pitching effects everything I do. It determines what I eat, where I go and what time I go to sleep at night." Most experts agree that pitching is 85% of the game. It would be ridiculous to assume that a pitcher comes out of the bullpen and begins to throw with no mental preparation. Yet this is an aspect of pitching which is largely ignored and must be taught, just as the physical mechanics of pitching are taught. *Good pitching begins on the bench. Know your hitters and use your time on the bench to study their strengths and weaknesses.*

ASSETS OF A WINNING PITCHER

A pitcher who wants to win consistently must:

1. Have good control.

2. Know how to field his position.

3. Analyze the hitters and know their strengths and weaknesses.

4. Have confidence in his ability.

5. Keep his body—especially his legs—in top physical condition.

6. Form good pitching habits.

7. Concentrate. Pick out a spot and throw to it.

8. Communicate with his catcher.

9. Think pitching and pitch thinking.

10. Practice and use "mental pictures".

11. Change speeds on the hitter.

12. Pitch *"in"*.

13. Work *fast.* *

*The game should be won or lost in two hours. The longer you hold the ball, the harder it is for the infielders to keep their concentration. Catfish Hunter, Tommy John, Ron Guidry, Steve Carlton, Don Sutton—the list goes on and on—all work *fast.*

70

THINGS A GOOD PITCHER SHOULD KNOW:

1. Stay ahead of the hitter.

2. Make the hitter hit your pitch.

3. Know your best pitch and use it when you're in trouble.

4. Have confidence.

5. Know your weakness and work hard to overcome it.

6. Know the game situation.

7. Know the importance of the outs and the runners on base.

8. Know who is covering what base.

9. Field all ground balls unless you're called off.

10. Control your temper; never argue with an umpire.

11. Keep control of yourself when errors are made behind you.

12. Pick up your target before making the pitch.

13. Be in control—be mean and aggressive.

14. Develop *one* style of pitching.

15. Follow through on all deliveries. This is a natural motion and will ease the strain on the pitching arm.

16. Back up plays from the outfield to 3rd and home.

18. Throw all pitches with the same motion.

19. Break for 1st on balls hit to the right side of the infield; be ready to take a toss at 1st if the 1st baseman is pulled away from the bag.

20. Throw curve balls around the knees; don't try to throw them high.

21. Know your hitters and watch for "keys"; some hitters will tip you off as to what they're looking for.

22. Throw high and hard in possible bunt situations.

23. Have an idea of what you're going to do on every pitch. Know the inning, score and count on every hitter *all the time.*

MENTAL PREPARATION FOR PITCHERS

Know your strengths and weaknesses. The number one rule in pitching is: "Never get beat with your second or third best pitch." This means that if you are in a situation where you can lose the game, don't let a hitter beat you on anything less than your best pitch. Of course, there will be days when you will not be effective with your "best" pitch, so you must feel confident with your second and third pitches as well. *Remember:* Situations vary. On a given day, your second or third best pitch may become your *best* pitch! A successful pitcher will recognize this.

A successful hitter in the Major Leagues will get a hit only 3 out of 10 times. With these odds, the pitcher already has a great advantage. Don't give the advantage back to the hitter by throwing him a pitch that you don't have complete confidence in.

Learn to control your emotions and actions. If an umpire misses a pitch, get the ball back and *don't dwell on the mistake.* Think *only* about the next pitch. The worst thing a pitcher can do in this situation is become upset with the umpire. Pitchers who consistently argue with umpires over called strikes develop reputations which encourage umpires to be hard on them. If the pitcher continually attempts to "show up" the umpire, he may take his frustration out on your team as a whole.

Pitchers who train themselves to regain their composure after a bad call (and this *does* take training), will gain the respect of the umpires. More often than not, this pitcher will "get" the close calls.

Catfish Hunter was one of the best pitchers I've ever seen in a situation where an umpire made a bad call. He would get the ball, get back on the mound and go after the hitter with a vengeance. By not showing up the umpire, he received more favorable calls than most. By keeping his emotions under control, Catfish did not allow the hitter at the plate to take advantage of the umpire's mistake by anticipating that an angry pitcher would throw anything less than his best pitch.

Learn to handle pressure. Many pitchers find that the pre-game warm up is the perfect time to prepare mentally for their job on the mound. They use this time to develop "mental pictures", in which they imagine themselves facing a particular hitter. Some even imagine the count and the game situation. In doing this, the pitcher is mentally prepared when the hitter comes to the plate. Many times, the pitcher actually finds himself in the very situation that he imagined in his visualization. Since he wisely used his warm up to anticipate the game situation, and actually "saw" the results he wanted to achieve, he is now ready to deal with it effectively.

The relief pitcher's approach to getting ready is different from a starter's because relievers must be ready every day. The reliever usually begins his mental preparation after infield practice. Early in the game, he begins to study the opposing hitters, anticipating which of them he may be brought in to face. He is *always* aware of the flow of the game. When he is called upon to "get loose", he is *mentally ready.*

Pitchers who feel good about their pre-game warm up can handle the pressure of a real game situation. They enter the game with a *positive mental attitude;* they feel confident because they know they are prepared.

If a pitcher loses his effectiveness on the mound, he is doing one of two things wrong: He has lost his concentration, or he has allowed himself to tense up. One usually leads to the other. *This is the time for him to get the ball, take a few deep breaths and concentrate only on the next pitch!* If this requires him calling a time-out, then he should do it.

Be aware of your mistakes, but don't dwell on them. Many pitchers try to be too smart; they're not content with just getting the hitter out—they try and embarrass him by making him look bad. In doing this, they often over-throw the ball. The result is that they may hang a curveball or throw the fastball over the heart of the plate, allowing the hitter to drive the ball. Another example is when the catcher may call for a pitch which isn't the one you wanted to throw. You throw it without having *total concentration*—you're thinking "I should be throwing a fastball, not a curve", when you should be thinking: "I'm going to throw my best curve and get this guy out." If the hitter hits your curveball, it's easy to lose your concentration and dwell on the catcher's mistake instead of bearing down on the next pitch so that you don't get yourself in a bigger jam. *A good pitcher will take control in this situation—he will shake off the catcher and take charge.*

The success of any pitcher is dependent upon the defense behind him. Avoid embarrassing your teammates by becoming angry when an error is committed behind you.

Like any infielder, I committed errors. When a pitcher stared me down, kicked the dirt, or otherwise tried to show me up, I became upset with him. Instead of concentrating on the next play, I would find myself dwelling on the fact that he had purposely gone out of his way to embarrass me. No one in the ballpark was more aware than I that I had made an error; I didn't need a pitcher to rub salt in my wound! By contrast, some pitchers will leave the mound and offer encouragement to the infielder who has misqued—as a result, the infielder recovers quickly and can give his full attention to the next play. By regaining your composure, you will win the respect of your teammates; they will compensate for the error by bearing down.

It is in the best interest of every pitcher to gain the respect of his defense. This will encourage them to make an extra effort when you pitch.

While you must be aware of these mistakes, you must not allow them to effect your pitching. The time to think about your mistakes is *after* the game. Put yourself back into the problem situation and think about what you *should have done, what you will do the next time, and what the positive results will be when you do the thing right.*

When a catcher calls a pitch you don't feel comfortable with, step off the rubber or shake him off—do whatever it takes to regain total composure. You may even want to call time out and talk with him.

Good pitchers are never satisfied—They are continually striving for improvement.

Mental practice can be the most effective tool a pitcher has. A pitcher's imagination can mean the difference between success and failure. It's a fact that mental practice can have the same results as physical practice. Form mental pictures of various game situations and visualize what you will do and what the positive results will be. "See" the hitter. "Hear" the cheers from the crowd as you strike him out. Be as specific as you can in your mental pictures and make them as real as possible.

PITCHING FORM

STANCE:

Pitchers should have a *balanced starting position,* either from the wind-up or the set; this is vitally important and effects the delivery and release of any pitcher. Relax on the mound, using as little energy as possible—avoid unnecessary pacing. *Take slow, easy breaths.*

WIND-UP POSITION—RIGHTHANDED PITCHER (RHP):

The first thing to remember is that the wind-up should be *simple.* Don't get too fancy, just stick to the basic mechanics outlined here. Don't exert undue energy in your wind-up which could be better spent in your delivery. Keep your head up, eyes focused on your target.

The RHP places the front half of his right foot on the rubber, with the left foot slightly behind it and to the side. His pivot foot should be near the RH corner of the rubber. This gives him the best angle to the right side of the plate and enables his breaking ball to hit the middle of the plate (hence, the outside corner) more often. In addition, it is more difficult for the hitter to see the pitch from this angle. Likewise, the lefthanded pitcher (LHP) should place his pivot foot near the lefthand corner of the rubber.

With his right arm relaxed at his side, the RHP has the ball deep in his glove as he takes the sign from the catcher. After receiving the sign, he puts his right hand over his glove-hand wrist and grips the ball palm-to-palm. From here, he brings both hands just above the bill of his cap, being careful not to bring them too far over his head (which would allow the hitter to see the ball). As both arms swing downward, he begins to pivot on his right foot, bringing his left foot and knee back to a position that is about even, or slightly behind, the pitching rubber. Now, he puts the ball and hand out of the glove, swings his right arm down and back, shifts his weight, comes forward, plants the ball of his left foot and heel in a direction straight at home plate and, with a quick arm action forward (a ¾ to overhand delivery), he releases the ball to the plate. *Keep the ball well hidden; the hitter shouldn't see it until the point of release.* At this point, he brings his right foot forward, and plants it beside his left, at least shoulder width apart. He is now in a crouched position and is prepared to field the ball.

SET POSITION—RHP:

In the set position, the RHP straddles the rubber, his back to the runner(s) on base. He moves into a set position with his foot in contact with the rubber, takes his sign and straightens up, bringing both arms into a set position. Now, he checks the runner(s) and begins a quick left-leg pivot. Keep the foot close to the ground and use the same motion as in the wind-up position. The right knee should be slightly bent while in the set position; your legs should never be stiff in the stretch.

Use the rubber as an aid to help you drive toward the plate in all positions.

THE GRIP:

The grip is individual to each pitcher and must be made comfortable through trial and error. There are some basic tips on the grip used in specific pitches which will be discussed later. *Caution: Your grip will sometimes reveal the type of pitch you are going to throw.* For example, some pitchers will turn their wrist in before throwing a curve ball, or their wrist will be facing the hitter before throwing a fastball. Smart hitters are quick to pick up these weaknesses and most certainly will take advantage of them. *Keep the ball well hidden until the time of delivery!*

THE NO WIND-UP DELIVERY:

In the no wind-up delivery, pitchers do not bring their hands over their heads before they pivot on the rubber. The no wind-up delivery is good for pitchers who have trouble keeping their balance when using the conventional wind-up technique. It is also useful to pitchers who have difficulty hiding the ball before delivery.

THE DOUBLE-PUMP WIND-UP:

Considered to be a useful tool when trying to break a hitter's concentration, the double-pump wind-up is basically the same as the conventional wind-up except that once the pitcher has his hands over his head, he drops them down and begins the wind-up again, rocking back on his back foot. This sometimes throws off a hitter's timing as well.

DELIVERY:

Pitching is not all arm strength. *It is a total body action.* Concentrate on keeping your shoulder tucked (left shoulder for RHP, right shoulder for LHP). Drive with your legs, *low and hard. Use the rubber* as a tool to aid you in driving toward the plate. Think *"low and hard"* as you release the ball. If you make a mistake up, it can mean a home run. A mistake low may only result in a ground ball.

THE FOLLOW THROUGH:

Once the weight has been transferred to the left leg, the right (back) leg should follow through and finish up almost in a direct line, and squared off to the plate. The upper body should be bent forward at the waist, helping to pull the arm down and across the body. The elbow should end up touching the area of the left thigh and the hand and wrist should be outside the left knee. The complete follow through will find the glove hand somewhere out in front of the body; the body should be squared off, preparing the pitcher to field his position.

CONTROL:

Unquestionably, the most important element in pitching is control. Foremost in achieving control is the pitcher's mental approach to the game. Once he has mastered a positive mental attitude and feels confident on the mound, he must then consider the physical aspects of control which he has learned.

Good control is the result of consistent use of pitching mechanics and techniques. A pitcher with good control is consistent in his rhythm and style of delivery.

PITCHING PROBLEMS AND SOLUTIONS

PROBLEM: Lack of concentration.

SOLUTIONS:

1. Study carefully the "Mental Preparation for Pitchers" in this book.

2. Pick up your target before beginning your wind-up. Keep your eye on the target until you release the ball.

3. Think *only* about the pitch you are *getting ready to throw*.

PROBLEM: Rushing the pitch.

SOLUTIONS:

1. *Relax.* Make sure you have good balance when taking the sign.

2. Don't move your body toward the plate too soon. There should be a slight bend of the knee on the pivot foot leg.

3. Don't step back too far with your non-pivot foot as you begin your motion into the wind-up.

4. Take a good, full pivot so the hitter can see your back pocket. For a RHP, the hitter should see your left pocket.

5. Concentrate on keeping your weight on your back leg.

PROBLEM: Throwing across the body.

SOLUTIONS:

1. The RHP should have the pivot foot near the RH corner of the rubber. The LHP should have his pivot foot near the LH corner of the rubber.

2. Draw a line from the pivot foot to and through the middle of home plate, making sure that the lead foot lands slightly to the left of that line.

PROBLEM: Improper arm action.

SOLUTIONS:

1. When removing the ball from your glove, make sure the palm of your hand is *down.*

2. Move your arms toward home plate, not toward 1st or 3rd base.

PROBLEM: Short arming (not using full arm action when throwing).

SOLUTIONS:

1. You may be rushing, or may not be getting a full back swing with your arm.

2. Are you recovering from an injury, or do you have a sore arm?

3. Have you been taught to use a *full* follow through?

PROBLEM: Control.

SOLUTIONS:

1. Check for rushing.

2. Are your basic pitching mechanics sound?

3. Do you have *total concentration?* Make sure you are *mentally prepared* before going to the mound.

PROBLEM: Loss of power on delivery.

SOLUTIONS:

1. Check your stride foot. Make sure you aren't opening up too much. The upper body should be closed until the arm has reached the top of the backswing and is moving toward the plate.

2. Drive *low and hard* toward the plate.

PROBLEM: Poor body balance.

SOLUTIONS:

1. Don't rock too far back on your wind-up or from the set position.

2. Are you rotating your hips far enough before delivery?

HOLDING RUNNERS ON:

The most important thing for a pitcher to remember with runners on base is: *never allow any baserunner to take a walking lead—it is up to you to stop him.* You do not want to appear "predictable" with runners on base. Remember to vary your moves and the number of times you pump. Vary the release point of your throw to 1st, and be aggressive in your efforts to hold the runner on. Know the game situation and the ability of the baserunner(s) at all times.

TAKING SIGNS:

1. Take signs from the rubber.

2. Relax.

3. Use your head and your glove to deceive the opposition.

4. Shake the catcher off if you are not comfortable with the sign.

5. Vary the number of times you pump; avoid forming patterns which will enable the hitter to predict what you are going to do.

6. After you have taken the sign, use your glove and body to hide the ball. The hitter shouldn't see the ball until delivery.

THE PITCHER AS A FIELDER:

A pitcher's job is just beginning when he delivers the ball. The importance of a pitcher as a good fielder cannot be overstressed. Frequently, a pitcher gets himself into trouble by his inability to field a ground ball. *A well pitched game can be lost by the pitcher's inability to field his position correctly.*

1. Field everything unless you are called off.

2. On balls hit to your left, break for 1st base. If necessary, cover the bag. Otherwise, stay out of the play.

3. Take all possible bunts. Break hard and "look" the ball into the glove before you try to throw it. Listen to the catcher—he'll tell you what base to throw to.

4. When a play is going to be made at 3rd or home, and runners are advancing, run half-way between the bases in *foul* territory before you decide which base to back up as the throw comes in.

THROWING TO 2ND FOR A DOUBLE PLAY:

1. Always know who is covering the base so that you can lead correctly. Usually it will be the SS, as it is an easier play for him to handle.

2. After you catch the ground ball, take a short shuffle step toward 2nd base. This will allow you to get your balance while giving the SS time to get to the bag.

3. Make a good, *chest high* throw to the infielder. *Don't overthrow the ball.*

THROWING THE BASIC PITCHES

THE FASTBALL:

There are two types of grips used in throwing the fastball:

1. Across the seams: The across the seams grip is primarily used by pitchers who want their fast ball to go at it's maximum velocity without much movement. Example: If you want to pitch a hitter up and in, you would want the ball to stay up and in. This pitch is used by power pitchers like Nolan Ryan and Rich Gossage. The ball is held across the seams, at the widest part, in order to achieve the four-seam rotation.

2. With the Seams: If a pitcher has problems getting his fastball to move, he can grip the ball with the seams. This grip is used by pitchers who want to sink the ball as well as make it move in and out.* Tommy John is a good example: He doesn't have an over-powering fastball, so he was forced to develop another pitch. He mastered the "sinker" and probably throws it at about 78 or 80 MPH. So you see, movement is sometimes more important than speed when throwing a fastball.

* Though gripping the ball at the seams will cause it to move more, it can also cause loss of velocity and control problems. Each pitcher should experiment with the grips to see which is best for him.

When throwing the fastball, the index and middle fingers should not be too far apart. If they are, the wrist will lock. This prevents the pitcher from getting the maximum velocity. If the fingers are too close together, severe control problems will result as the ball can easily slide off the fingers as it is released. The ball should be gripped firmly, but not too tight, and as far toward the fingertips as possible. If you hold the ball too far back in your hand you will restrict your fingers and wrist from their full range of motion; this will result in loss of velocity. *You should see light between your palm and the ball.*

THE SINKING FASTBALL:

If thrown properly, this is an ideal pitch to use in a DP situation, as it usually produces a ground ball. The sinker should be thrown with the fingers on the seams and a ¾ to side-arm motion. This will allow your wrist to turn over slightly as the ball is released. *Apply pressure with the index finger as the ball is released. Drive low and hard and stay on top of the ball.* The sinker is a difficult pitch to master because of the arm motion needed.

82

However, if it is thrown properly, it is one of the most effective pitches a pitcher can throw.

THE CURVE BALL:

The curve ball can make or break a pitcher. If a pitcher doesn't have an effective breaking pitch the hitter will ignore his breaking ball and sit on his fastball. I don't care how hard a pitcher can throw, good hitters can eventually time your fastball and hit it hard. A curve is used to fool the batter, to disrupt his timing and keep him off balance. If thrown correctly, the curve should not put a strain on the pitcher's arm. Young pitchers should use caution when throwing these pitches before they are physically mature enough. I think age fourteen is about the right time for young pitchers to begin experimenting.

When throwing the curveball, the grip should be firm, but not too tight. Only the thumb and first two fingers should be used in throwing the curve. The ring and little finger should be bent into the palm. Any pressure by the ring or little finger will reduce both speed and rotation of the ball. The elbow should *always* be above the shoulder. The throwing shoulder must be above the lead shoulder. By doing this, you will be releasing the ball down-hill. If the lead shoulder is higher than the back shoulder, the pitcher will have a difficult time getting on top; this results in the pitcher throwing a flat curve instead of a sharp curve.

The stride is shorter when throwing a curve than it is with a fastball; this enables the pitcher to get on top of the pitch. He must follow through completely so he can maintain the arm velocity necessary to "snap off" a good curve. In addition, a good follow through, with the arm coming across the body, helps the pitcher get into a good fielding position.

TIPS FOR THROWING A GOOD CURVE:

1. Don't try to throw it too hard.

2. Pull *down* on release, as if you are lowering a window shade.

3. Put pressure on the middle finger and thumb.

4. Use your index finger as a guide.

5. Keep your elbow *up* and parallel with your shoulder.

6. Cock your wrist. Poor wrist action will cause the ball to lose proper rotation.

7. Don't grip the ball too tightly or have it too far back in your palm. This will effect the spin. The loser the grip, the slower the curve.

8. Follow through, slapping yourself in the back.

9. Bring your hand and arm down on the opposite side of your throwing arm.

10. "Snap" your wrist.

11. Warm up slowly to get the proper spin.

12. Stay on top of the ball.

13. Keep your non-throwing shoulder in.

THE CHANGE-UP:

It requires a great deal of timing to hit a change-up. A properly thrown change-up makes a fastball appear to be traveling faster than it is, so it disrupts the hitter's timing. That is why the change-up is so effective. Throwing it is easily taught—the difficult part is getting the confidence to use it.

As the ball tends to travel high in the strike zone, a low release point is essential. Though a change-up does not have to be thrown at the knees to be effective, a ball low within the strike zone is less likely to be hit out of the ballpark. There are three commonly used grips:

1. The palm Ball: The ball is held back in the palm of your hand. Fingertips are raised slightly as you release the ball. Most of the pressure should be on the second row of knuckles on the first two fingers. On release, the hand is *behind the ball,* not on top.

2. Three Fingers: Some pitchers feel they get better control if they grip the ball with three fingers instead of two. By using three, you create a greater drag, which causes the ball to slow down.

3. Off Center: With the off center grip, you hold the ball with the middle and ring fingers on top. The thumb and index finger are held on the inside of the ball, touching slightly and forming a small circle. The little finger is held on the outside of the ball.

On all three grips, when the ball leaves your hand, the hitter should not be able to detect that a change-up will be thrown.

All of your actions—hand, wrist and arm—should indicate to the hitter that you are going to throw a fast ball. The grip and release of the change-up help to slow the velocity. Your wrist must be "dead"; there should be no "snap" as there is when you throw a fastball. The elbow on your throwing arm must be kept higher than your shoulder. This is to keep your change-up from getting too high in the strike zone. Try and hit home plate with the ball.

85

THE SLIDER:

When properly thrown, the slider will break faster and flatter than a curve ball. It should look like a fastball coming at the hitter and then break at the last second. As the slider doesn't break as hard as a curve, it is an easier pitch to throw for strikes. However, if not thrown correctly, the slider becomes a pitch that can hurt you because it is thrown with less velocity than a fastball. Instead of breaking, it can stay right where you throw it.

The slider has earned a reputation as a pitch which frequently causes arm problems for pitchers who use it. Sparky Lyle, one of the greatest relief pitchers of all times—and a master at the slider— feels that this reputation grew because most pitchers don't throw the slider correctly. They throw it across the body instead of staying on top of the ball and behind it. When Sparky finished, he tried to follow through so his left arm would finish under his right.

Sparky gripped the slider with no seams. This way, when he entered a game, he didn't have to worry about finding a ball with "good seams"; he could devote his entire concentration to his delivery and the rotation of the ball.

Some pitchers grip the slider the same way as the fastball except that they hold it *slightly* off center with the middle and index fingers placed to the *outside* of the ball. The index finger should be next to a seam with your thumb on a seam underneath the ball. The fingers and thumb should not grip the ball too tightly until the second of release. *Maximum pressure is placed on the ball with your middle finger.* To achieve tight spin on the slider, grip tightly with the index and middle fingers on release and "snap" the wrist just as you would when throwing a fastball.

86

The middle finger generates the spin which makes the ball slide. *Fingers must remain on top of the ball and slightly off center as the hand moves to the release point.* If your fingers move too far down on the side of the ball your slider will be slow and flat. *Don't turn your wrist inward as you release the ball.* This action will flatten out your slider and put *extreme pressure* on your elbow. Concentrate on a *full follow through* in order to get the maximum velocity.

CATCHING

The catcher is the pulse of a good defense. The other eight players will take their cues from you. You must be energetic and enthusiastic; you must *take charge of the defense and hustle 100% of the time.* You must *know the hitters:* First-ball hitters, good curveball hitters, etc. You have to know what each hitter is looking for when he comes to the plate. You must *know the pitcher.* What pitches are working for him? If he's not effective with his number one pitch, you have to be aware of that. Don't let him be too fine; you can't catch a walk!

1. Wear protective cup and helmet during BP, while in the bullpen, and during the game.

2. *Always* wear a catcher's mask when warming up pitchers.

3. During BP, protect your bare hand behind your back or knee. If you want to throw through to 2nd base, tell the batter to swing and miss. That way, you can receive the pitch and throw it properly without fear of a foul tip. Don't throw to 2nd more than 3 or 4 times in succession.

4. Don't catch BP on one knee; a foul tip on the thigh is painful and you won't be 100% for the game.

5. Catch as close to the hitter as you can. Foul tips will hit your glove more often.

6. Never use a new glove in a game.

7. Catch *every pitch.*

8. When giving signs, have your toes pointed straight ahead before crouching; this will keep your knees in and block your signs from

the opposing coaches.

9. Use your glove to hide signs even more; check with your 1st and 3rd basemen—if they can see your signs, so can the coaches.

10. Go from the sign to the receiving position in the same way on every pitch. Some catchers will move the right foot first on breaking pitches and the left foot first on fastballs; the opposition will pick this up.

11. Hold the bare hand loosely in a fist with the thumb inside the cup formed by the fingers.

12. Be ready to receive when the pitcher begins his wind-up. Don't give the sign, then stand up and go back into the receiving position. The pitcher will be half way through with his delivery and still won't have a target to aim at.

13. Anticipate a stolen base on every pitch. *Don't wait until you catch the ball to get your body into throwing position.*

14. *Don't jump up* as you catch, or you'll lose a lot of strikes for your pitcher.

15. Your glove should always move *toward* your body as you catch the pitch. Don't push low balls toward the ground or corner pitches away from the plate.

16. Check the defense before giving signs. You are the only player who can see the entire defense—know where you want every player to be. Don't hesitate to move players if they are out of position.

SHIFTING:

Shifting helps you get your body in front of the pitch and gets weight to your right foot for a throw. It's hard to get velocity on a throw without pushing off with your right foot. Shifting should be forward as well as lateral in order to get your body moving in the direction of the throw. It isn't necessary to shift on pitches you can catch between your shoulders; just keep your right foot planted and step toward your target with your left foot.

You should be in the process of shifting, or almost finished, *by the time you catch the ball.* On an outside pitch (righthanded hitter), step with the right foot to the right and forward as you catch the ball. Step toward your target with the left foot as you throw. With a lefthanded hitter, move your left foot first, to the left and forward as you catch. Plant the right foot behind the left as you step toward your target with your left foot.

THROWING:

1. Keep wrist and fingers upright. This will give you riding fastball rotation and helps eliminate throws which sink, tail or slide.

2. Try to grip the ball across the seams to obtain *four-seam* rotation. This will give your throw more carry and greater accuracy.

3. Always throw to the bag on stolen bases; it's the infielder's responsibility to get there.

4. When throwing to 3rd on a stolen base, throw *over* a righthanded hitter when possible. Otherwise, clear yourself from the hitter.

5. To throw to 3rd in front of a RH hitter, (pitch outside, or outside corner), step to the right and forward with the right foot.

6. To throw in back of a RH hitter, (most strikes and inside pitches) step behind him with the left foot. Bring the right foot behind the left, plant and throw.

BUNTS:

1. Call the fielder and the base to throw to on *all* bunts. *Call with authority!*

2. Field bunts with *both hands.* Use your glove to push the ball into the open, bare hand.

3. Get your body in position to throw before you field the ball.

4. On bunts to 3rd, circle to your left to get your body moving toward 1st as you field the ball. If the ball is stopped or moving slowly, you can bare-hand it and pivot away from the infield to make the throw.

5. With a runner on 1st and the 3rd baseman fielding the ball, it's the catcher's responsibility to cover 3rd.

POP-UPS:

1. *Go after every pop-up!*

2. All pop-ups curve toward 2nd base.

3. Try to have both feet planted and still before catching the ball. This will keep your head still and the ball won't seem to "bounce" so much.

4. Hold on to your mask until you are positive where the catch will be made. Then, *toss it in the other direction.*

TAG PLAYS:

Most tag plays at home are missed because the catcher doesn't catch the throw. During infield practice, wear your mask and shinguards while taking throws from the outfield; stay in there and catch every throw.

1. Avoid collisions whenever possible. Give the runner part of the plate to aim for.

2. If the runner isn't sliding, go meet him up the line if possible. "Give" with the tag as you spin toward home plate.

3. If a collision is unavoidable, *be ready.* Have your body low and make certain that your weight is *forward.*

4. When tagging a sliding runner, *point your left toe directly at him.* If your toe is pointing left, the inside of your knee is exposed and injury may occur. If it's pointing to the right, the outside of the knee is vulnerable.

BLOCKING BALLS:

With a pitch in the dirt and the runner stealing, you must try to catch the ball in order to have any chance at the would-be stealer. However, if there is a runner at 3rd, you must block the ball to keep the run from scoring.

The blocking position is on both knees, arms at your side (this makes you wider), chest squared to the pitch and your upper body curved forward to keep the ball in front of you. Blocking balls is a learned reaction, mastered only through a lot of practice. You can't become proficient at it merely by thinking about it—you have to get dirty!

Most low balls get past the catcher between his knees. *You must drop both knees at the same time and use your glove to cover the space between them.* Keep your glove on the ground and don't try to catch the ball. On balls in the dirt to your right or left, move forward as well as laterally. This will keep your chest squared to the pitch and the ball won't carom off to the side. *Be sure that you land on your knee.* If you shift on your foot first, the ball will be past you.

Because of the rotation, a RHP's breaking ball will kick toward your glove hand; the LHP's will kick toward your bare hand.

THE 1ST BASEMAN

STANCE AND FOOTWORK:

You should have movement toward the hitter as the pitcher releases the ball. As the ball passes the hitting zone, weight should be on the balls of your feet. Your legs should be shoulder-width apart, hands relaxed belt-high in front of you. Your eyes should be clearly focused on the hitting zone.

Break hard on all ground balls. *Don't watch the ball—find the bag.* Your body should face in the direction of the ground ball. Always set the same way with the same foot on the bag; preferably, corner-to-corner with your right foot on the right corner of the bag and your left foot on the left corner.

When a fielder releases the ball, stretch out as far as possible with the lead foot to catch the ball. *Don't stretch too early.* Use the crossover step to stretch on a ball opposite the glove-hand side. Keep your feet off the top of the bag; use the front corners as guideposts. Use either the right or left corner when you stretch, or use the middle on a good throw. Come off the bag on errant throws.

Make sure all runners tag the base.

POSITIONING AND CUT-OFFS:

The 1st baseman has three positions to take, depending on the game situation:

1. Back Position: With a lefthanded hitter and no chance of a bunt, make sure to get off the line so a step and a dive will cover it.

2. Half-way: Possible bunt situation, with a good bunter and fast runner. With a righthanded hitter get half-way, then move 3 or 4 steps to the right.

3. In Position: A definite bunt situation and a possible play at home with a runner on 3rd base.

Trail runners to 2nd base on extra base hits. *You are the cut-off man on extra base hits* if there is a runner on 1st. On a cut-off from CF, take the throw on top of the mound to prevent a bad hop off the rubber or mound. On a cut-off from RF, get deep toward the catcher and come back toward the throw.

Make a decision on all throws, considering the runner, the game situation and the type of throw. Use your best judgement, make your own decisions, and don't depend on the catcher for instructions.

Signal that you are the cut-off man by raising your arms high above your head and waving.

HOLDING RUNNERS ON:

1. Stay in fair territory.

2. When breaking off the bag, take a crossover step, then two shuffles with your knees bent. Take your glove to the ground with your eyes focused on the hitting zone.

3. Give a low target when holding runners on base.

4. Make a *firm tag* on your runner on *every* throw to the bag.

5. Alert the catcher when a runner goes.

CATCHING THE BALL:

1. Field from the ground up, low to high.

2. Catch the ball in the web.

3. Use *one* hand, except when blocking the ball.

4. On a throw into the runner, make the tag while "giving" with your arm to avoid injury. Let the runner tag himself out.

5. Always anticipate a bad throw.

6. On balls in the dirt, use soft hands and "give" with the glove toward your body. Start with your glove on the ground; make adjustments up.

7. On balls in the dirt with a runner at 2nd, *block the ball.* Come *off* the base on a wild throw.

8. Block ground balls to 1st with your body if necessary; you can still throw the runner out.

9. You may have to slide to the back part of the base on some

long hops and high throws.

10. *Don't overcharge.* Stay back and get a big hop, especially with runners in scoring position.

11. On foul balls, go to the fence and then work back.

12. Call off the catcher on pop-ups.

13. When the ball gets away from the catcher on the 3rd strike, give a good target, either inside or outside, depending on where the ball goes.

THROWING:

1. Give the pitcher the ball early.

2. *Get one out in all DP situations* where you throw to 2nd base. *Don't rush the throw;* let the SS turn the double play.

3. In a DP situation, *Don't throw across the runner.* Stay inside or out and throw for the SS's head. Don't watch the play, get back to the bag.

COMMUNICATION:

1. Tell the pitcher to get over with a lefthanded hitter.

2. Tell the 2nd baseman when you move and where you are playing.

3. On balls to your right, go as far as possible, then yield to the 2nd baseman. *Know your 2nd baseman's range!*

4. Have the 2nd baseman alert you to curve balls and change-ups.

5. Keep infielders alert by reminding them of the number of outs and the situation.

6. Remind the 3rd baseman of who is the cut-off man.

95

PLAYING THE INFIELD

JUMPS AND STANCE:

A phrase often applied to a well-fielded ball is that the infielder "got a great jump on it". The best infielders get better jumps because they know how to get ready (stance). Not all infielders are built alike. If you're 6'2" tall, you won't be able to get as low, or "bent" at the knees as a player who is 5'6"; you'll have to have a more upright stance. Your physical makeup and the position you play will determine which stance is best for you.

In the *proper stance,* feet should be shoulder-width apart. Weight is on the balls of the feet, hands are relaxed, about belt-high. Knees are slightly bent, back should be straight and head toward the hitter.

Infielders who get consistent good jumps have good lateral movement. If a player has poor lateral movement, he should check the following things:

1. Are his feet too close together?

2. Is he leaning too far forward? On his toes?

3. Is his weight on his heels?

4. Is he standing too upright?

5. Is he bent too much at the knees or at the waist?

SLOW ROLLERS:

If an infielder is having trouble handling slowly hit balls, he may be catching the ball off of the wrong foot. The correct way to field a slow roller is off of the *right* side. The fielder *breaks hard* for the ball. Just before he gets to the ball, he should slow down enough to get his balance and shift his body so he can field the ball off of his right side. His right foot should be back. Fielding the ball on the right side enables the fielder to throw the ball with one step and allows a quicker release because the ball is already on his right side. *If the ball is rolling with any speed at all, catch it with your glove. If it's setting down in the grass, bare-hand it in exactly the same way—off of your right side.*

A good drill for a 3rd baseman who's having trouble fielding slowly hit grounders is to get him back and hit him some slow rollers. *He should charge hard.* A common mistake among 3rd basemen is that they don't break hard in the beginning; they play too cautiously and then try to force the play. *Charge hard at first and then slow down to get control of your body.*

THE BACK-HAND:

When teaching infielders to back-hand the ball, stress the importance of keeping the left foot in front when catching the ball. This enables them to field the ball cleanly, take one step with their right foot, plant and throw. Catching the ball off of the right foot forces the fielder to take a step with his left foot and then his right. The result is that the fielder takes one, and sometimes two too many steps. (For 3rd basemen, this technique isn't always possible due to the velocity of the ball.)

STIFF HANDS:

A player who has "stiff hands" usually isn't relaxed and may not be as confident as he should be regarding his fielding ability. Here again, mental practice can prove invaluable. *Visualize* yourself in various fielding situations and *imagine positive results.*

If a player has stiff hands, he should check for the following things:

1. He may be "stabbing" at the ball instead of catching it. He should take some ground balls without his glove on; this will help him develop soft hands. Imagine that the ball is an egg—it should be caught with the hands out in front and very relaxed.

2. Is he overcharging?

HANDCUFFING:

"Handcuffing" is a term used when a player lets the ball get too close to his body before it makes contact with his glove. A player who is consistently handcuffed is probably doing one of the following things wrong:

1. He's letting the ball "play him". He should work on charging the ball while keeping his body under control. By charging the ball, he can choose the best possible hop.

2. He may be pounding his glove just before he attempts to catch the ball. This is a bad habit for a young player to get into. More often than not, he will pound his glove late; this will cause him to "stab" at the ball. Stabbing causes stiff hands, which causes handcuffing.

3. He may have his hands too close to his body. This causes him to be played by the ball. *He must keep his hands out in front and close to the ground. It's easier to come up for the ball than to go down after it.*

PIVOT AT 2ND BASE:

Successful execution of the double play is one of the most valuable defenses in the game. In order to execute the pivot at 2nd accurately, a 2nd baseman must do the following things:

1. Get to the bag early.

2. Get your body under control.

3. Bend at the knees and lower your center of gravity—this one thing alone will help keep your body under control.

4. Keep your hands soft and relaxed. *Let the ball come to you— don't reach out and get it.*

5. Always face the person you are receiving the ball from.

6. *Pivot:* Unless you are straddling the bag, you should always try to put your *left foot* on the bag. This enables you to come across the bag, plant your right foot and throw. On a ball up the middle, take the throw from the SS, plant your right foot and throw.

A good 2nd baseman knows *Different ways to turn a double play:*

1. Straddle: Self-explanatory.

2. Across the Bag: This method is usually used on a ball hit toward 2nd base where the SS can under-hand the ball to the 2nd baseman. This type of pivot helps the 2nd baseman get more on his throw.

98

The 2nd baseman places his left foot on the bag, just as he is receiving the ball. His right foot crosses over the bag and plants about 10" from it. He pivots on the right foot and throws to 1st base. *The 2nd baseman should not commit too soon; not all throws will be perfect.*

3. Step Back: Left foot on the bag. After receiving the throw, step back with your right foot, plant and throw.

4. Left Foot on the Bag: Follow the ball up the middle, facing the SS. Take the throw, almost like a 1st baseman, plant your right foot and throw.

THE SS AND THE DOUBLE PLAY:

The pivot for the shortstop is as follows:

1. Face the person you are receiving the throw from.

2. Have your body under control. Bend at the knees and lower your center of gravity; this will help you slow down.

3. Have your arms and hands relaxed and away from your body.

4. Let the ball come to you—*don't* reach out and grab it.

5. Give a target with your glove and right hand.

6. Stay behind the bag; you can adjust more easily if the throw is bad.

7. Touch the bag with your *right* foot. The only time you might tag it with your left is when you are taking the throw from the 1st baseman on the *inside* of the baseline.

8. *Use two hands.*

COVERING THE BASES ON A STEAL:

Depending on who's covering the bag, the 2nd baseman or the SS must cheat in his position by coming in and over on the pitch. Taking two short steps toward the baseline before breaking for the bag will allow him to cover his ground.

99

THE TAG PLAY:

The tag play at 2nd for a 2nd baseman is simple: You merely straddle the bag.

The SS has two options on a tag play: He can straddle the bag, or he can place his left foot up against the home plate side of the bag. In this method, he *must* let the ball come to him; if he gets in the habit of reaching for it, and the baserunner gets under his tag, *he should straddle the bag.* The advantage in placing your left foot inside the bag is that it allows you to move up the line and out of the way of the sliding baserunner while still enabling you to take the throw from the catcher and make the tag.

SUMMARY

A GOOD INFIELDER KNOWS:

1. The stretch of his arm and how deep he can play.

2. The SS and the 2nd baseman must cheat toward 2nd to turn the DP effectively.

3. The speed of the runner.

4. The atmospheric conditions: Wind, sun, type of playing surface.

5. A good infielder knows where the outfielders are playing and how far to go out for a relay play. He knows the strength of the outfielder's arms.

6. Who is batting and how will he be pitched?

7. Who covers the bag on a steal?

8. Who covers the bag on balls hit back to the pitcher?

9. What bag do you cover in the following situations: Bunt? Relay? Pick off?

10. Know the infield fly rule: An infield fly is a fair fly ball (not including a line drive or a bunt) which can be caught by an infielder with ordinary effort. The ball is alive and runners may advance at the risk of the ball being caught, or retouch and advance after the ball is touched. *If a declared infield fly is allowed to fall untouched to the ground, and bounces foul before passing 1st*

or 3rd base, it is a foul ball. The infield fly rule is in effect with runners at 1st and 2nd, or bases loaded and one or no outs. If the ball goes into the air and, in the umpire's judgment, the infielder can catch the ball, he will signal the infield fly rule. After the fielder makes contact with the ball, the runners may advance at their own risk.

11. Exchanging runners: In case of a run down, always try to get the runner out of scoring position; get the fastest runner off base.

12. The obstruction rule: Obstruction occurs when a runner interferes with an infielder while he's in the process of fielding the ball. If no play is being made on an obstructed runner, the play will proceed until no further action is possible. The umpire will call time and impose such penalties as, in his judgment, will nullify the act of obstruction.

13. The interference rule: Offensive interference is an act by the team at bat which interferes with, obstructs, hinders or confuses a fielder attempting to make a play. If the umpire declares the batter, batter-runner or a runner out for interference, all other runners shall return to the last base that was, in the judgment of the umpire, legally touched at the time of interference.

PLAYING THE OUTFIELD

A good outfielder is smart, alert to all game situations, and hustles every minute. He backs up every throw and base hit possible, always assuming the infielder will miss the ball. He hustles 100% of the time and always knows when and where to throw the ball.

A good outfielder knows the following things:

1. The score.

2. The importance of the tying and winning run.

3. The count.

4. The type of hitter at the plate.

5. The speed of the infielders when going back on fly balls.

6. The infielder's weaknesses in moving right and left.

7. The strengths and weaknesses of the other outfielders in his unit.

8. The type of pitcher.

9. The speed of the runner.

10. How the ball rebounds from the fence and screen.

11. Atmospheric conditions and condition of the playing surface.

12. Which outfielder is in the best position to take the ball, pivot and throw?

13. The sun field.

14. The outfielder is in charge when it comes to running an infielder off the ball.

15. Back up the bases when bunts, pick-off plays, stolen bases and rundowns are in order.

16. A good outfielder knows when to catch a foul ball and when to let one go.

17. Know the warning track and the ground rules.

A good outfielder should *never:*

1. Chase ground balls on his heels.

2. Flip his sunglasses down before he locates the ball.

3. Catch the ball on the side when throwing.

4. Catch fly balls flat-footed when throwing to get the runner out.

5. Overcharge the ball when throwing.

6. Catch low line drives with his glove facing down.

7. Throw behind the runner.

8. Play all hitters the same depth.

9. Lift his head and watch the runner before fielding the ball. (You should "watch" the ball into your glove before you pick up your target.)

10 Run with the glove arm extended until the last step or two prior to the catch.

11. Miss the cut-off man.

12. Give up too soon on a fly ball.

13. Catch a ball one-handed when it's possible to catch it with two.

BASIC OUTFIELD DRILLS

CHARGE DRILL:

Begin by hitting five easy ground balls. Gradually hit them harder. After fifteen to each player, move them back 15-20 feet. Now, one at a time, each player charges the ball and attempts to catch it in front of the original 45' marker. This drill is particularly effective for players who hesitate when charging the ball.

THROW FROM THE MOUND:

Have the outfielder throw from the mound with particular emphasis on the break point. Keep his front shoulder down and turned in. Also emphasize a long throw and make sure he is throwing over the top. As the mechanics of throwing from the outfield are much the same as those of pitching, your pitching coach will be helpful in this drill. This is a good exercise for outfielders who tend to open up too soon and/or throw out over their front foot.

BREAK DRILL:

Designed for players who get a slow break on balls to either side or over their heads. Stand 10' from the player with a ball in each hand. Toss balls under-handed to the right and left, noticing if the player crosses over on the first step. Whenever possible, the player should get in good catching position and get the ball out of his glove as if making a throw. Some balls will be tossed directly over his head or shoulders. In these instances, you're looking for the player to make a drop-step rather than a cross over.

LONG TOSS:

Each outfielder should long-toss two or three times a week. Players should pair off, throwing softly from about 60' and gradually (5 minutes) work out to 200-250'. Throws should be kept on an arc, with no more than five throws being made at the maximum distance. A good drill for stretching the arm muscles and increasing the length of the throws.

FENCE DRILL:

The key to this drill: Outfielders must communicate during the play. Hit long fungoes to the fence in the gaps. One player must try for the catch while the other has to get in position to play any carom off the fence. Another part of the fence drill is hitting balls over the player's head. Have him find the fence, then come in or over to make the catch.

ALL PURPOSE DRILL:

This is a daily drill that all the outfielders should do after throwing in infield practice. All throws should be short and at a designated spot (a hat) on the ground. This will help keep the throws over the top and the release point out in front. Do this drill as follows:

1. Base hit directly at outfielder with no one on base.

2. Base hit directly at outfielder with runner on 1st.

3. Base hit to the player's left.

4. Base hit to the player's right.

5. Fly ball to player's left.

6. Fly ball to player's right.

7. Fly ball over the player's head.

8. Line drive hit at the player.

9. Base hit directly at the player with the winning run on 2nd base.

DO THIS DRILL EVERY DAY!

INFIELD GROUNDERS:

Outfielders who have bad or hard hands should take ground balls *every day* with the infielders.

CATCH AND RELEASE:

Release time can be speeded up if the player learns to catch a fly or ground ball with a low center of gravity. This is achieved by having him keep his rear-end down as he is making the catch; he's already getting his legs and shoulders into the optimum throwing position. If done correctly, he should be able to throw with only two steps after the catch.

USING SUNGLASSES:

Besides learning how to use glasses properly, the player must learn to block the sun with his glove or bare hand. Throw or hit balls directly into the sun. Each player should learn to look away from the sun by turning sideways or even by turning his back to the infield.

105

PICK-OFF AND RUN DOWN PLAYS

Runners on 1st, 1st and 2nd, or bases loaded—1st baseman behind the runner*

RHP: He gets the sign, comes set and looks back to 2nd. When he sees the 1st baseman break, he turns and throws to 1st base, giving a not-too-hard *chest high throw.*

LHP: The pitcher gets the sign and comes set. When he lifts his leg, the 1st baseman races toward the bag and makes the tag. The throw should be the pitcher's best move, *chest high,* and not too hard.

*The 1st baseman must not play too deep.

THE DAYLIGHT PLAY—RUNNERS AT 2ND, 1ST AND 2ND, OR BASES LOADED:

The SS moves into a position behind the runner. When he feels the runner is far enough off the bag, he flashes an open glove so the pitcher can see it, and then breaks hard for the bag. The pitcher then wheels and throws a chest high throw over the bag. *The pitcher must give the SS a throw he can handle!*

THE PICK-OFF PLAY WITH THE 2ND BASEMAN:

This play is given by the 2nd baseman to the pitcher: The 2nd baseman closes his glove or wiggles his glove fingers. The pitcher acknowledges the sign by tapping his foot on the rubber; the 2nd baseman then alerts the CF that the play is on so he can charge.

The pitcher comes set, checks the runner. When he turns his head toward home, the 2nd baseman races to the bag. The pitcher wheels and throws a *chest high throw.* The CF is charging hard. *It is imperative that the pitcher gets the sign!*

THE 3RD TO 1ST PICK-OFF PLAY:

Done by RHP's only! Runners at 1st and 3rd, pitcher gets the sign from the 3rd baseman. Again, the sign used is a wiggle of the glove.* The pitcher acknowledges the sign by tapping on the rubber. *The 3rd baseman is the key to this play.* The pitcher comes set, steps toward 3rd. If the 3rd baseman's hands are down, the pitcher wheels and throws back to 1st. If his hands are up, he is telling the pitcher that the runner at 1st has broken for 2nd. The pitcher then wheels and locates the runner. *The pitcher should not hold the ball too long.*

THE WHEEL PLAY AT 2ND BASE:

The SS gives the sign to the pitcher. (The sign is a circular movement of the index finger on the throwing hand.) The pitcher acknowledges the sign by tapping on the rubber. The SS alerts the CF by placing his glove on the back of his head. The pitcher comes set, checks the runner at 2nd. When he lifts his leg, the SS breaks toward 2nd; the CF races in and the pitcher turns back toward 2nd. He *doesn't wheel around,* as in his normal move. (Example: The RHP wheels to his *right,* the LHP wheels to his *left.*) He gives the SS a *chest high throw.* This play is used with runners at 1st and 2nd, 2nd and 3rd, or with the bases loaded. It's a great play when the count is 3-and-2 and the runners are going.

*You will notice that, in most cases, the "signs" are not given. This was done to encourage each team to develop their own system for giving signs. Signs are easily picked up by the opposition so, obviously, each team's should be different.

107

DEFENSIVE ASSIGNMENTS

Men on 1st & 2nd—man on 1st is picked off

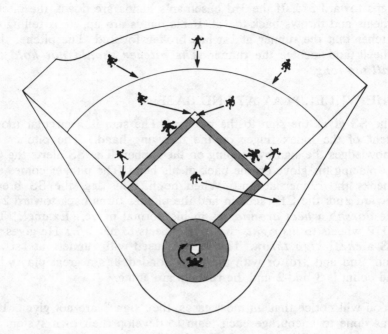

P: Back up 1st.

C: Cover home.

1ST. Cover 1st; be the tag man.

2ND: Cover 2nd; be the run-down man.

SS: Back up and cover 2nd with the possibility of being run-down man and tagger.

3RD: Cover 3rd to keep runner on 2nd from advancing.

RF: Come in to help back up 1st base.

CF: Help back up 2nd.

LF: Help back up 2nd.

Men on 1st & 2nd—man on 2nd is picked off

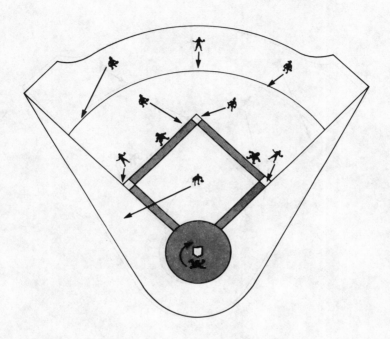

P: Back up 3rd.

C: Cover home.

1ST: Cover 1st.

2ND: Cover 2nd, with possibility of being run-down man and tagger.

SS: Cover 2nd; be tag man.

3RD: Cover 3rd; be the run-down man.

RF: Back up 2nd.

CF: Back up 2nd.

LF: Back up 3rd.

Men on 1st & 3rd—man on 3rd is picked off

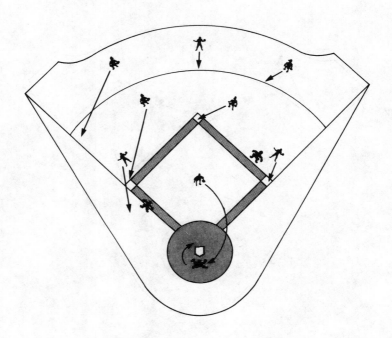

P: Cover home, back up catcher.

C: Cover home; be
run-down man.

1ST: Cover 1st to keep the
runner from advancing.

2ND: Cover 2nd; keep runner
on 1st from advancing.

SS: Back up 3rd.

3RD: Cover 3rd; be the tag man.

RF: Back up 2nd.

CF: Back up 2nd.

LF: Back up 3rd.

RUN DOWN—INFIELD IN
(The follow-in play by the 3rd baseman.)

Man on 3rd tries to score on ground ball to the infield—infield is in

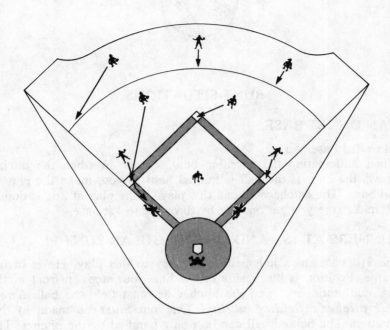

P: Cover home.

C: Cover home; be the
run-down man.

1ST: Cover 1st.

2ND: Cover 2nd.

SS: Cover 3rd.

3RD: Follow about 10' behind
runner off 3rd to make a quick
tag; keep the batter from
going to 2nd base.

LF: Back up 3rd.

CF: Back up 2nd.

RF: Back up behind 1st base.

111

BUNT SITUATIONS

MAN ON 1ST BASE:

1st or 3rd baseman:
When anticipating the sacrifice bunt, charge in when the pitcher throws the ball. If the ball is bunted hard to you, make the play to 2nd base. The catcher will call this play. If the play at 2nd is doubtful, make sure you get one out by throwing to 1st base.

RUNNERS AT 1ST AND 2ND—REGULAR BUNT PLAY:

The 3rd baseman's judgment is the key to this play. He is in full charge. Position is just inside of the line, four steps in front of the bag, and stationary. Tell the pitcher he must field the ball. *Know your pitcher's fielding ability!* One out *must* be made in this situation. The bunted ball can be easily handled by the pitcher. The 3rd baseman covers the base without taking his eyes off the ball. Tag the base with your right foot for better balance; be in position to make the throw to 1st.

On balls bunted down the line, the 3rd baseman charges the ball and runs the pitcher off. The play to 1st base is much easier for the 3rd baseman in this situation.

RUNNERS ON 1ST AND 2ND—USED IN LATE INNINGS:

This is a designed play and must be controlled by a sign. The pitcher, 1st baseman and 3rd baseman charge toward the batter. The SS shortens the distance, then races to cover the 3rd base bag. The 2nd baseman bluffs the runner, then covers 1st.

CHARGE PLAY:

Runner at 1st, RHP: He comes set, lets the 1st baseman take two steps toward home, then delivers a strike with something on it.

112

Runner at 1st, LHP: He comes set, lets the 1st baseman take two steps, then delivers a strike with something on it. The 1st baseman should be at least half-way before the ball is bunted. The sign used is the bill of the hat. *The 1st baseman must make sure the pitcher has the sign.* If he doesn't acknowledge the sign, call time out and tell him!

THE PICK-OFF PLAY IN A BUNT SITUATION:

This works better with a lefthanded pitcher and is usually used late in the ball game with the bunt in order. *RHP:* He comes set, lets the 1st baseman take two steps toward home, then turns and throws a *Chest high throw* to the 1st baseman. This is a *timing play* and must be practiced!

LHP: This is an outstanding play and should be used frequently. The pitcher comes set, allows the 1st baseman to take two steps toward home, and then gives his *best move* toward 1st. This is also a *timing play* and must be practiced! *The 1st baseman must make sure the pitcher has the sign.*

THE PICK-OFF IN A BUNT SITUATION WITH MEN ON 1ST AND 2ND:

Play #1: Use regular bunt defense.

Play #2: Pick-off at 2nd base: The pitcher comes set, lets the SS break toward 3rd. The 3rd baseman takes two steps toward home and so does the 1st baseman. The 2nd baseman breaks when the pitcher (after checking the runner) turns his head toward home. *Timing is essential;* this must be *practiced.* The 2nd baseman must cheat a little toward 2nd. He must also alert the center fielder that a pick-off play has been called.

THE RUN DOWN PLAY:

Important: Always run the runner back to the bag from which he came!

Try to start this play when the runner is half-way between the bases. Give the ball to the forward man and let him run the runner back to the base from which he came. The forward man should run hard at the runner, but not with a fake motion of the arm. The tagger should stay in front of his bag, and inside the baseline. This will give him the proper angle for the throw.

When the runner is about 10' from the tagger, the tagger should make a *break* toward the runner. This is the sign to the thrower that he should give the ball to the tagger on his first step. The thrower makes an *easy, chest-high toss.* When the play is executed correctly, one throw is all that's needed to get the runner at any base. The man without the ball must avoid interfering with the runner.

REMEMBER:

1. *Run the runner back to the bag from which he came.*

2. *Run the runner hard.*

3. *The tagger and the thrower stay inside the baseline.*

4. *The tagger must stay in front of his bag until making his break.*

5. *The thrower should make an easy, chest-high toss. Don't throw quick and hard!*

DEFENSIVE ASSIGNMENTS

BUNT SITUATIONS

Runner on 1st

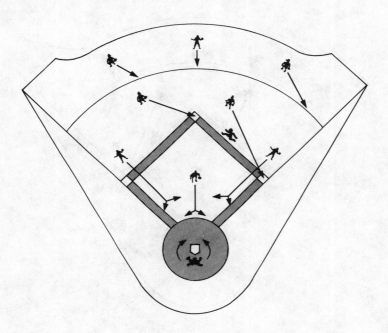

P: Break toward the plate after delivering the ball.

C: Field all bunts possible; *call the play.* Cover 3rd when 3rd baseman fields the bunt close to home.

1ST:* Cover the area between 1st and the mound.

2ND: Cover 1st; shorten position.

SS: Cover 2nd.

3RD: Cover area between 3rd and the mound.

RF: Back up 1st.

LF: Move in toward 2nd base.

CF: Back up 2nd.

*Lefthanded first baseman: Charge toward home, staying close to the foul line. *Always keep the bunted ball to your right.*

Runners on 1st & 2nd

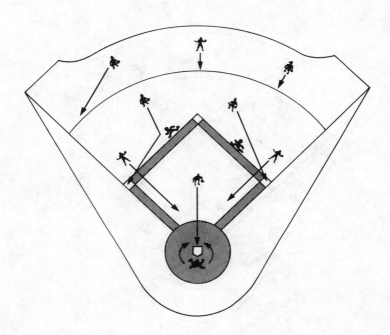

P: Break toward the plate.

C: Field bunts in front of plate or *call the play.*

1ST:* Charge toward the plate.

2ND: Bluff the runner, cover 1st base.

SS: Shorten distance toward 3rd. Get closer to the line, just over the shoulder of the runner, then race to cover 3rd.

3RD: Charge toward home.

Outfielders: Move to the infield area on *all* bunt situations.

Righthanded first baseman: Charge the bunted ball, keeping it to your left. This is done by charging toward the mound, then looping to your left.

116

Runners on 1st & 2nd

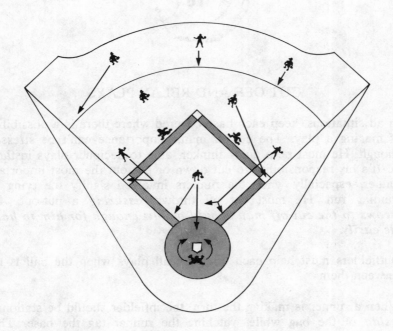

P: Break toward 3rd base line upon delivering the ball.

C: Field bunts in front of the plate; *call the play.*

1ST: Be responsible for all balls in the area between 1st in a direct line from the mound to home.

2ND: Cover 1st.

SS: Hold runner close to the bag before the pitch; cover 2nd.

3RD: Take position on the edge of the grass; *call the play,* whether the pitcher or 3rd baseman is to field the bunt.

RF: Back up 1st.

CF: Back up 2nd.

LF: Back up 3rd.

Your first objective is to retire the runner at 3rd, but one runner *must* be retired.

CUT OFF AND RELAY PLAYS

In all situations, keep each base covered where there is a possibility of making a play. The cut-off man's importance can't be stressed enough. He must be a quick thinker, able to decipher plays instantly. It's his responsibility to cut down or put out the most important runner, especially when the runners involved signify the tying or winning run. He must cut off throws, *assuring* a put-out. *All throws to the cut-off man should be low enough for him to handle easily.*

Outfielders must help each other on all plays when the ball is hit between them.

When a runner is making the turn, the infielder should be stationed *inside* of the bag while watching the runner tag the base. This makes the runner take a wider turn and increases the distance he must travel toward the next base. *Don't interfere with the runner by being too close to the base.*

CUT-OFF ASSIGNMENTS:

FOR THE 1ST BASEMAN:

You are the cut-off man on all base hits and fly ball scoring situations to *right and center field except* in these situations:

1. Single to right field between 1st and 2nd basemen with a runner on 2nd.

2. Single to right field between 1st and 2nd basemen with runners on 1st and 2nd.

3. A double, or possible triple down the right field line with a runner on 1st.

When 1st base is occupied, you are the cut-off man on *all extra base hits, except* when you have a double or possible triple down the right field line with a runner on 1st. In this situation, you are a trailer.

FOR THE 2ND BASEMAN:

You must cover 1st on these situations:

1. Single to right field with a runner on 2nd.

2. Single to right field between 1st and 2nd.

3. Single to right field between 1st and 2nd basemen with runners on 1st and 2nd.

FOR THE 3RD BASEMAN:

You are the cut-off man in these situations:

1. Single to left field with runner in scoring position.

2. Single to left field with runner in scoring position, judgment play, the throw should go to 2nd base.

3. Fly ball situations to left field with a runner on 3rd base.

FOR PITCHERS:

You are the cut-off man in two situations:

1. Pop fly in right field area.

2. Pop fly in left field area.

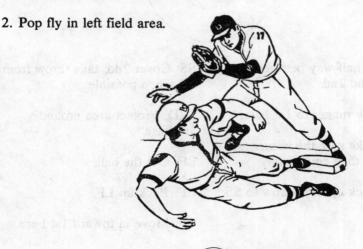

119

11

DEFENSIVE ASSIGNMENTS

SINGLE TO LEFT FIELD

No one on base

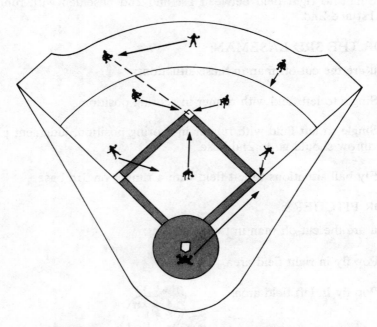

P: Move half-way between mound and 2nd.

C: Follow runner to 1st base.

1ST: Make sure the runner tags the base, then cover 1st.

2ND: Back up Lf's throw to SS.

SS: Cover 2nd; take throw from LF when possible.

3RD: Protect area around 3rd base.

LF: Get the ball.

CF: Back up LF.

RF: Move in toward 1st base.

SINGLE TO LEFT FIELD

Man on 1st

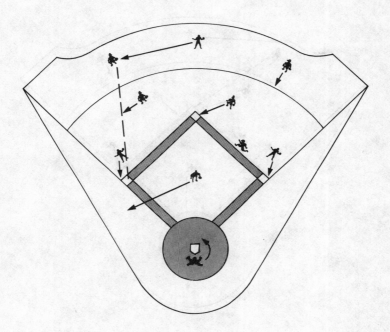

P: Back up 3rd.

C: Protect home.

1ST: Cover 1st.

2ND: Cover 2nd.

SS: Move into position to be cut-off man on throw to 3rd base.

3RD: Cover 3rd.

CF: Back up LF.

RF: Move in toward the infield.

SINGLE TO LEFT
(This is a judgment play.)

Man on 2nd, hitter is tying run

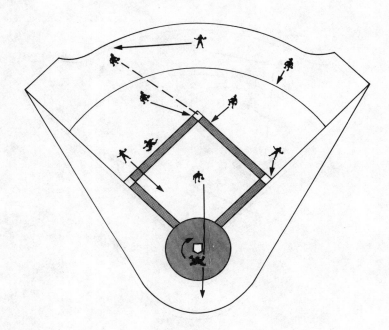

P: Move off mound to back up home in case the LF'er makes the throw to the plate.

C: Cover home.

1ST: Cover 1st.

2ND: Back up 2nd.

SS: Cover 2nd base.

3RD: Move to position to be cut-off man in case the LF throws home.

LF: Make low throw to 2nd to keep the batter from advancing to scoring position.

CF: Back up LF.

RF: Help back up 2nd base.

Never let the tying run into scoring position at 2ND base by making a foolish throw to the plate!!

122

SINGLE TO LEFT
(Ball hit between SS & 3rd base)

Man on 2nd, or 2nd & 3rd

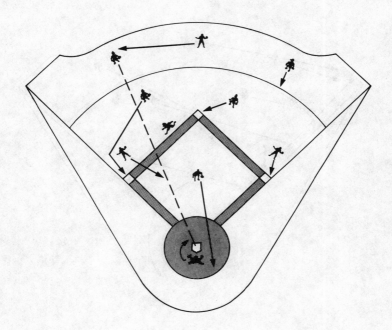

P: Back up home.

C: Cover home.

1ST: Cover 1st.

2ND: Cover 2nd.

SS: If the 3rd baseman can't recover, you become cut-off man. Otherwise, cover 3rd base.

3RD: Cut-off man. Take position about 45' from home in line with the LF'er and home plate.

LF: Throw to the plate.

CF: Back up LF.

RF: Back up 2nd.

DOUBLE, POSSIBLE TRIPLE
DOWN LEFT FIELD LINE

Man on 1st

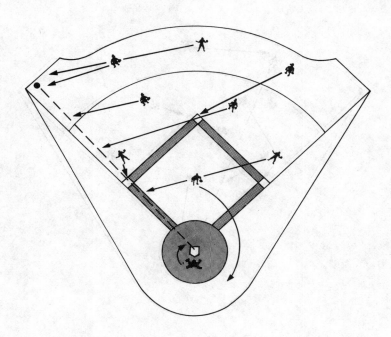

P: Back up home.

C: Cover home.

1ST: Cut-off man.

2ND: Become trailer behind the SS.

SS: Relay man.

3RD: Cover 3rd.

LF: Get the ball.

CF: Back up LF.

RF: Cover 2nd.

DOUBLE POSSIBLE TRIPLE
TO LEFT CENTER
No one on, man on 2nd or 3rd,
or men on 2nd & 3rd

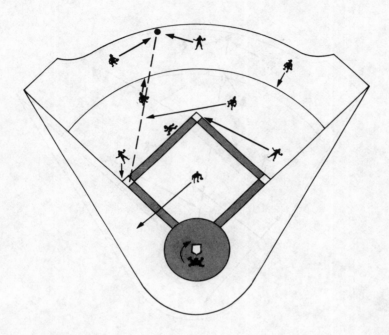

P: Back up 3rd in line with throw.

C: Protect home.

1ST: Trail runner to 2nd, cover the bag. Be ready for a play if the runner rounds the base too far.

2ND: Trail 30' behind the SS in line with 3rd.

SS: Go to a spot in left center; become the relay man.

3RD: Cover 3rd; stand on left side of the bag.

LF: Get the ball.

CF: Back up LF.

RF: Move in toward 2nd base.

DOUBLE, POSSIBLE TRIPLE TO LEFT CENTER

Man on 1st, 1st & 2nd, or bases loaded

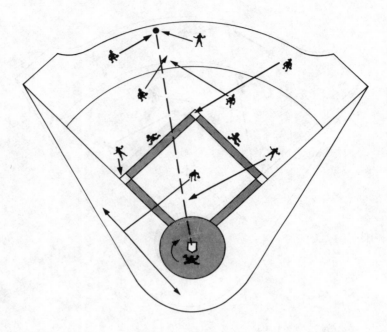

P: Go half-way between home and 3rd, then back up the base where the throw is going.

C: Protect home.

1ST: Cut-off man.

2ND: Trail 30' between the SS in line with 3rd base.

SS: Go to a spot in left-center and be the relay man.

3RD: Cover 3rd; stand on left side of the bag.

CF: Back up LF.

RF: Cover 2nd.

SINGLE TO LEFT FIELD

Man on 2nd, 1st & 2nd, or bases loaded

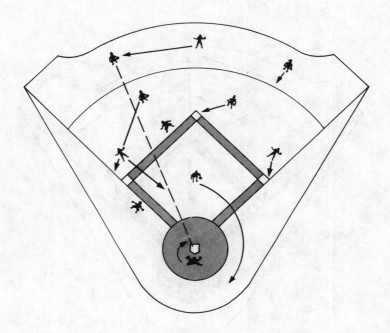

P: Back up home.

C: Cover home.

1ST: Cover 1st.

2ND: Cover 2nd.

SS: Cover 3rd.

3RD: Cut-off man.

CF: Back up LF.

RF: Move in toward 2nd base.

SINGLE TO CENTER FIELD

No one on base

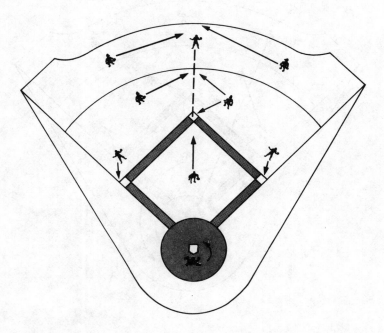

P: Move half-way between the mound and 2nd base.

1ST: Make sure the runner tags the bag, then cover 1st.

2ND: Back up the CF's throw to SS, then cover 2nd.

SS: Follow the ball, take the throw from the CF'er. You should be 30-40' from the bag.

3RD: Protect 3rd.

CF: Get the ball.

RF & LF: Back up the CF'er.

SINGLE TO CENTER

Man on 1st

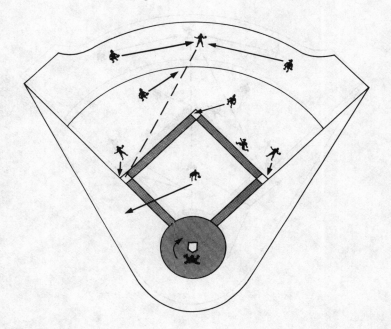

P: Back up 3rd.

C: Protect home.

1ST: Cover 1st base.

2ND: Cover 2nd base.

SS: Cut-off man on throw from CF to 3rd.

3RD: Cover 3rd base.

LF & RF: Back up CF.

SINGLE TO CENTER FIELD

Men on 1st and 2nd or bases loaded

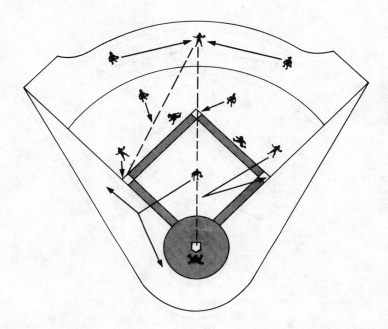

P: Go half-way between home and 3rd, then back up the base where the throw is going.

C: Cover home.

1ST: Move into a spot 45' from home in line with the throw; be the cut-off man. If throw goes to 3rd, go back to cover 1st.

2ND: Cover 2nd base.

SS: Cut-off man for possible throw to 3rd base.

3RD: Cover 3rd base.

LF: Back up CF.

RF: Back up CF.

SINGLE TO CENTER FIELD

Man on 2nd, men on 2nd & 3rd

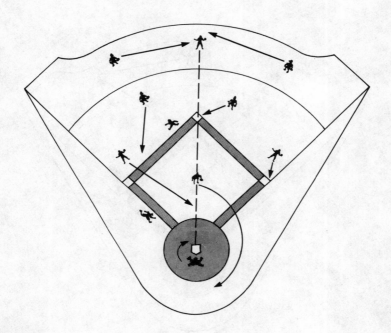

P: Back up home.

C: Cover home.

1ST: Cover 1st.

2ND: Go after the ball; then go back and cover 2nd.

SS: Go after the ball; then trail the runner to 3rd.

3RD: Cut-off man.

LF: Back up CF.

RF: Back up CF.

131

SINGLE TO RIGHT FIELD

No one on base

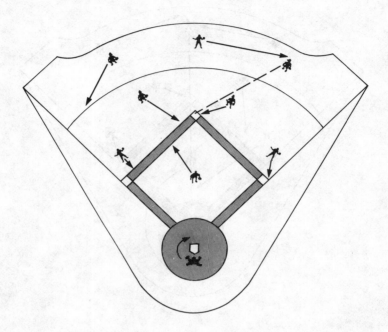

P: Move half-way between the mound and 2nd base.

C: Protect home.

1ST: Make sure the runner tags the bag when making the turn, then cover 1st.

2ND: Cover 2nd to take throw from RF.

SS: Back up RF throw to the 2nd baseman.

3RD: Protect 3rd.

CF: Back up RF.

LF: Move in toward 3rd base.

SINGLE TO RIGHT FIELD

Man on 1st, or 1st & 3rd

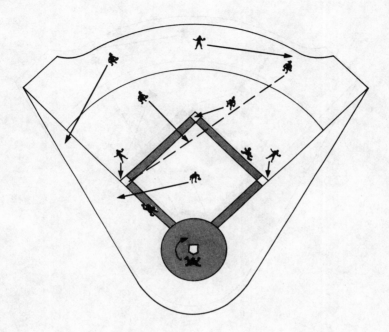

P: Back up 3rd, in line with the throw.

C: Protect home.

1ST: Cover 1st. Make sure the runner tags the bag.

2ND: Cover 2nd. Make sure the runner tags the bag.

SS: Station yourself about 45' from 3rd base, in a direct line from 3rd to the outfielder fielding the ball.

3RD: Cover 3rd.

LF: Move toward 3rd.

CF: Back up RF.

SINGLE TO RIGHT FIELD

Man on 2nd, men or 2nd & 3rd

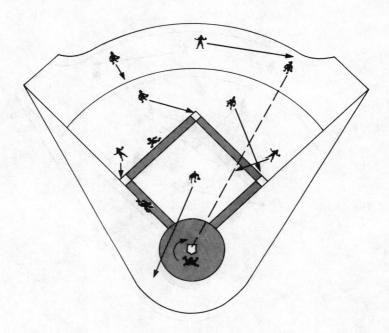

P: Back up home.

C: Cover home.

1ST: Go 45' from home plate to become cut-off man.

2ND: Cover 1st.

SS: Cover 2nd.

3RD: Cover 3rd.

LF: Move in toward 2nd base.

CF: Back up RF.

SINGLE TO RIGHT FIELD
(Between 1st & 2nd)

Men on 1st & 2nd, or bases loaded

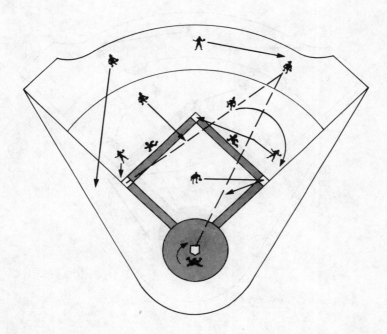

P: Start to cover 1st, when the ball goes through, retreat to be the cut-off man.

C: Cover home.

1ST: When you can't field the ball, go on and cover 2nd.

2ND: When you can't field the ball, go on and cover 1st.

SS: Cut-off man for possible throw to 3rd base.

3RD: Cover 3rd.

LF: Move into area behind 3rd to back up.

CF: Back up RF.

135

SINGLE TO RIGHT FIELD
(Between 1st & 2nd basemen)

Man on 2nd, or men on 2nd & 3rd

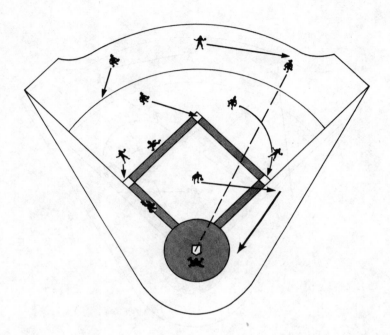

P: Start to cover 1st, then back up home plate

C: Cover home.

1ST: After attempting to field the ball, become the cut-off man.

2ND: After attempting to field the ball, continue to cover 1st base.

SS: Cover 2nd.

3RD: Cover 3rd.

LF: Move into the area behind 3rd.

CF: Back up RF, move in toward 2nd after the ball is fielded.

136

SINGLE TO RIGHT FIELD

Men on 1st & 2nd, or 1st, 2nd & 3rd

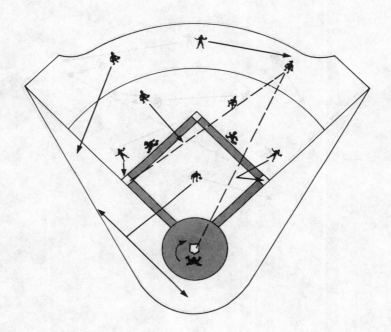

P: Go half-way between 3rd and home to see where the throw will go.

C: Cover home.

1ST: Cut-off man if throw is made to the plate. If throw goes to 3rd, cover 1st.

2ND: Cover 2nd.

SS: Cut-off man for throw to 3rd base.

3RD: Cover 3rd.

LF: Move to a point near the line and back up 3rd base.

CF: Back up RF.

RF: Make a low throw to the SS to keep the tying or winning run from going to 3rd.

Always keep the tying run from going to 3rd with less than two out. Give the opposing teem two runs to keep the tying run at 2nd. *Never make a foolish throw to the plate!*

DOUBLE, POSSIBLE TRIPLE
DOWN RIGHT FIELD LINE

No one on

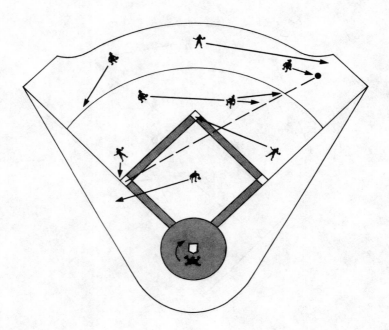

P: Back up 3rd.

C: Protect home.

1ST: Trail runner to 2nd base.

2ND: Relay man.

SS: Trail relay man.

3RD: Cover 3rd.

LF: Move into area behind 3rd base.

CF: Back up RF.

DOUBLE, POSSIBLE TRIPLE
DOWN RIGHT FIELD LINE

Man on 1st

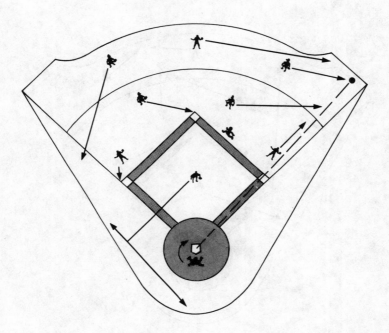

P: Go half-way between 3rd and home to see where the throw is going.

C: Cover home.

1ST: Trail 2nd baseman; stay about 30' behind him.

2ND: Relay man. Go to a spot in RF along the foul line, in line with the RF'er and home.

SS: Cover 2nd.

3RD: Cover 3rd.

LF: Move in toward 3rd base.

CF: Back up RF.

DOUBLE, POSSIBLE TRIPLE TO RIGHT CENTER FIELD

No one on, man on 3rd, or men on 2nd & 3rd

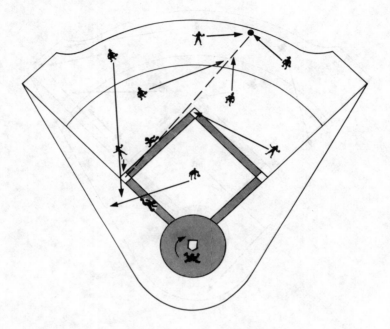

P: Back up 3rd, get as deep as possible.

C: Protect home.

1ST: Trail runner to 2nd, cover the bag. Be ready for a play at that base.

2ND: Go to a spot in CF (in line with 3rd) to become relay man.

SS: Trail 30' behind the 2nd baseman, in line with 3rd base.

3RD: Cover 3rd.

LF: Move in toward 3rd.

RF: Back up CF.

140

DOUBLE, POSSIBLE TRIPLE, TO RIGHT CENTER

Man on 1st, & 2nd, or bases loaded

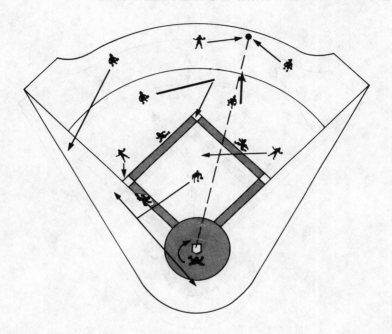

P: Go half way between 3rd and home to see where the throw is coming, then back up either base.

C: Cover home.

1ST: Cut-off man.

2ND: Relay man.

SS: Trail relay man then return to cover 2nd base.

3RD: Cover 3rd.

LF: Move into area behind 3rd base.

RF & CF: Go after the ball.

POP-FLY SITUATIONS

FOUL HIT BEHIND THE PLATE

Runners on 1st & 3rd, less than 2 out. Both runners tag up; runner on 1st breaks for 2nd. If there's no cut-off man, the runner on 3rd will score when the catcher makes his throw to 2nd.

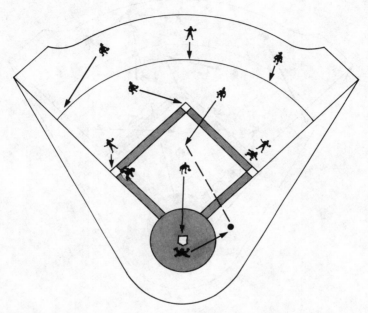

P: Cover home.

C: Catch pop-up; throw to cut-off man.

1ST: Help on pop-up.

2ND: Cut-off man behind the pitcher's mound.

SS: Cover 2nd.

3RD: Cover 3rd base.

LF: Come in, help back up short and 3rd.

CF: Back up 2nd.

RF: Cover 1st base.

POP-FLY HIT BEHIND 1ST BASE

Runners on 1st & 3rd, no outs; both runners tag up. The runner on 1st breaks for 2nd.

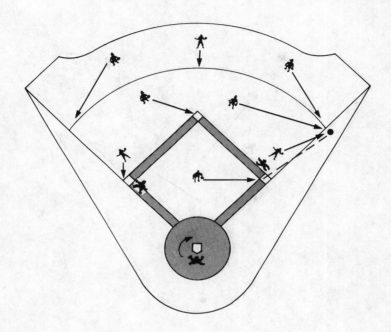

P: Come to a point near 1st base and be the cut-off man.

C: Cover home.

1ST: Catch the pop-up; throw to pitcher.

2ND: Also go after pop-up, then hustle to cover 1st.

SS: Cover 2nd.

3RD: Cover 3rd.

LF: Move to area behind 3rd for back-up man.

CF: Back up 2nd.
RF: Move in, help catch the pop-up.

143

DEFENSIVE ASSIGNMENTS

WILD PITCHES AND PASSED BALLS
Runner on 3rd, 1st, & 3rd or Bases Loaded

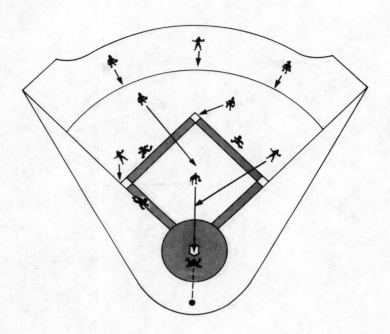

P: Cover home plate.

C: Retrieve the ball.

1ST: Back up home plate.

2ND: Cover 2nd base.

SS: Back up behind the mound.

3RD: Cover 3rd base.

Outfielders: Move toward the infield area to help where needed.

NOTES

NOTES

NOTES

NOTES

NOTES

Please send me_____copies of THE COMPLETE INSTRUCTIONAL BASEBALL MANUAL. I have enclosed $9.95 per copy, plus $1.00 per copy for postage and insurance.

NAME_____

ADDRESS_____
       (Number)   (Street)

_____
(City)   (State)   (Zip)

I WOULD LIKE INFORMATION ON QUANTITY DISCOUNTS_____

SEND CHECK OR MONEY ORDER TO:

THE COMPLETE INSTRUCTIONAL BASEBALL MANUAL
THE STANLEY COMPANY, INC.
8711 EAST PINNACLE PEAK ROAD
SCOTTSDALE, ARIZONA
85255

Please allow two weeks for delivery. Arizona residents add 6% sales tax.